FOR ORGANS, PIANOS & ELECTRONIC KEYBOARDS

E-Z PLAY® TODAY

189

IRISH FAVORITES

ISBN 978-0-7935-2174-6

7777 West Bluemound Road P.O. Box 13819 Milwaukee, WI 53213

Believe Me If All Those Endearing Young Charms

Registration 9
Rhythm: Waltz

3

The Galway Piper

Registration 2
Rhythm: Rock or Pops

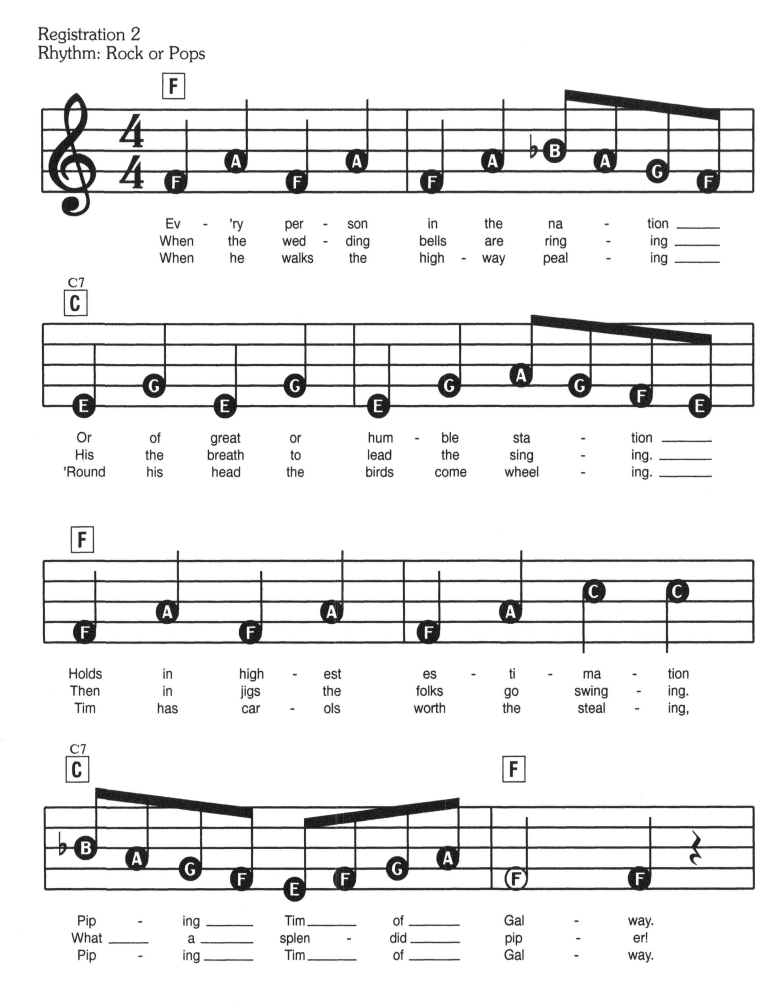

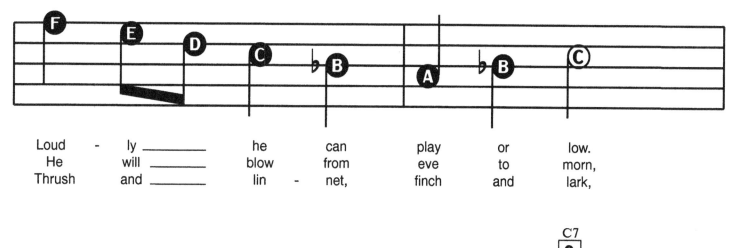

Loudly ____ he can play or low.
He will ____ blow from eve to morn,
Thrush and ____ lin-net, finch and lark,

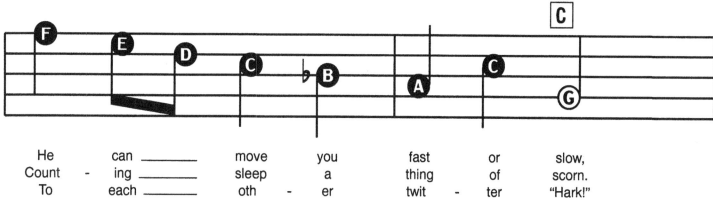

He can ____ move you fast or slow,
Count-ing ____ sleep a thing of scorn.
To each ____ oth-er twit-ter "Hark!"

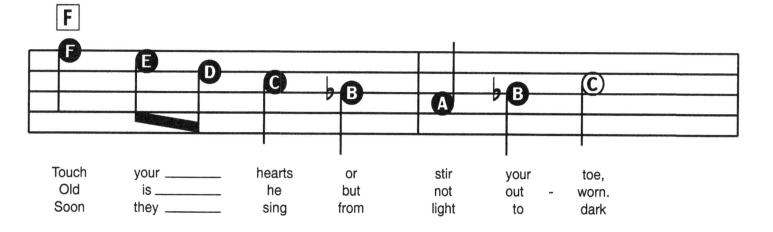

Touch your ____ hearts or stir your toe,
Old is ____ he but not out-worn.
Soon they ____ sing from light to dark

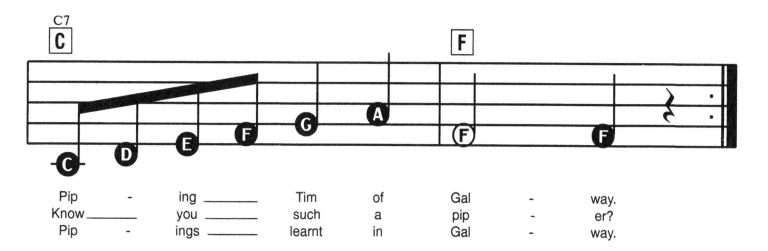

Pip-ing ____ Tim of Gal-way.
Know ____ you ____ such a pip-er?
Pip-ings ____ learnt in Gal-way.

Garryowen

Registration 9
Rhythm: 6/8 March

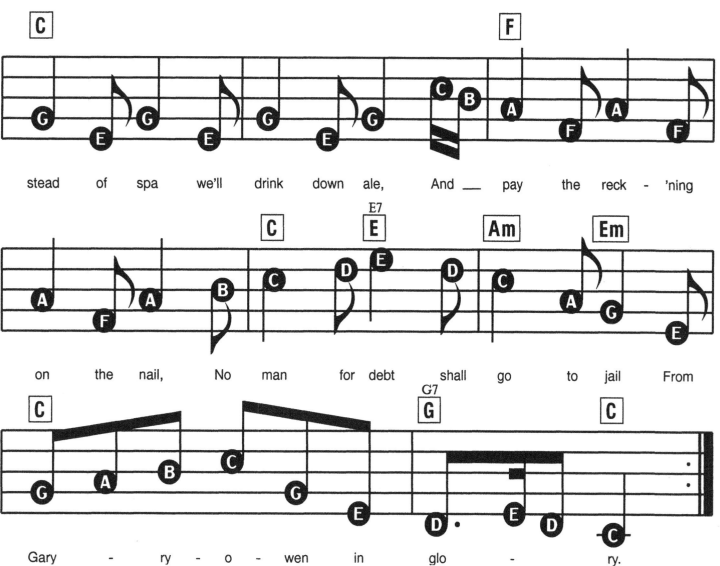

stead of spa we'll drink down ale, And __ pay the reck - 'ning on the nail, No man for debt shall go to jail From Gary - ry - o - wen in glo - ry.

Additional Lyrics

2. We are the boys that take delight in
   Smashing the Limerick lights when lighting.
   Through all the streets like sporters fighting,
   All tearing all before us.
   (Chorus:)

3. We'll break the windows, we'll break the doors,
   The watch knock down by threes and fours;
   Then let the doctors work their cures,
   And tinker up our bruises.
   (Chorus:)

4. We'll beat the bailiffs out of fun,
   We'll make the mayors and sheriffs run;
   We are the boys no man dares dun,
   If he regards a whole skin.
   (Chorus:)

5. Our hearts so stout have got us fame,
   For soon 'tis known from wence we came;
   Where'er we go they dread the name
   Of Garryowen in glory.
   (Chorus:)

The Girl I Left Behind Me

Registration 10
Rhythm: Rock or Pops

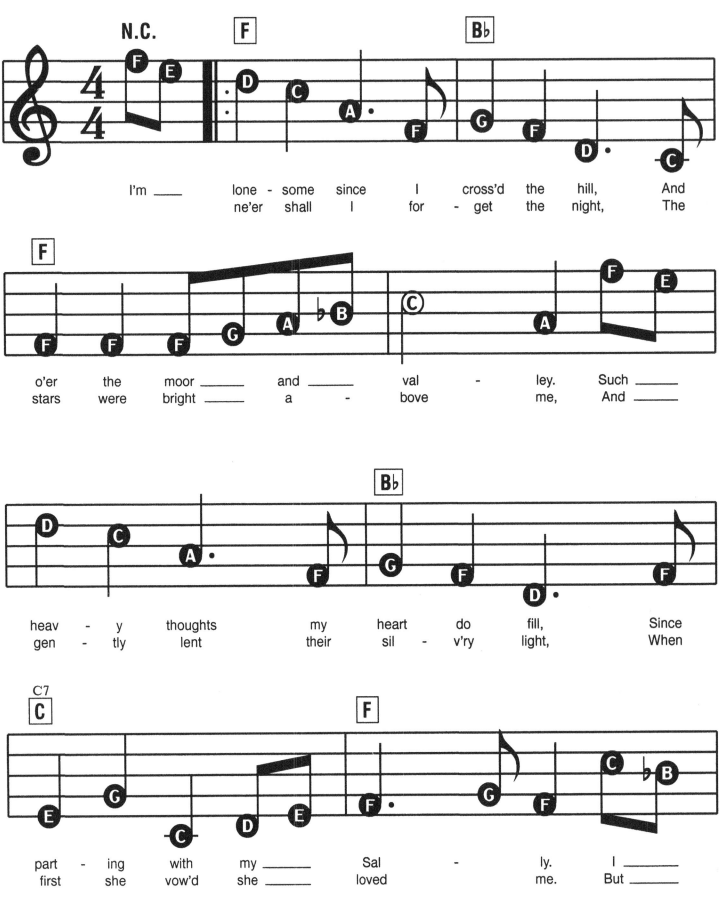

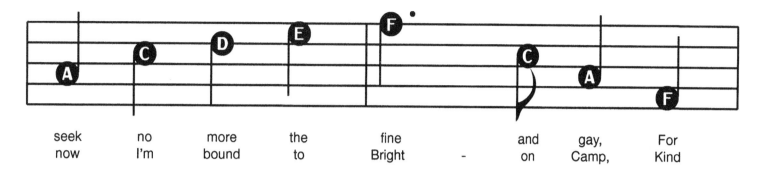

seek	no	more	the	fine		and	gay,	For
now	I'm	bound	to	Bright	-	on	Camp,	Kind

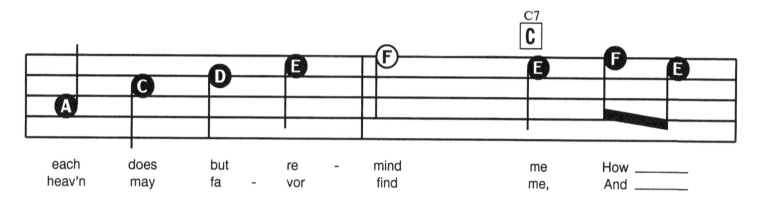

each	does	but	re	-	mind		me	How _____
heav'n	may	but	fa	-	vor	find	me,	And _____

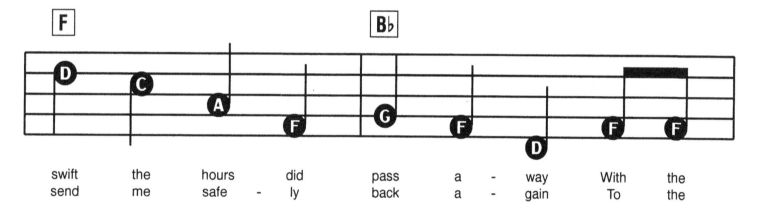

swift	the	hours	did	pass	a	-	way	With	the
send	me	safe	-	ly	back	a	-	gain	To	the

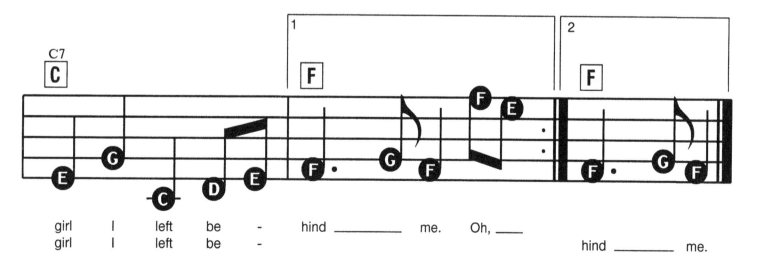

girl	I	left	be	-	hind _____	me.	Oh, _____
girl	I	left	be	-		hind _____	me.

The Harp That Once Thro' Tara's Halls

Registration 3
Rhythm: Pops or 8-Beat

Words by
Thomas Moore

Harrigan

Words and Music by
George M. Cohan

Registration 5
Rhythm: March

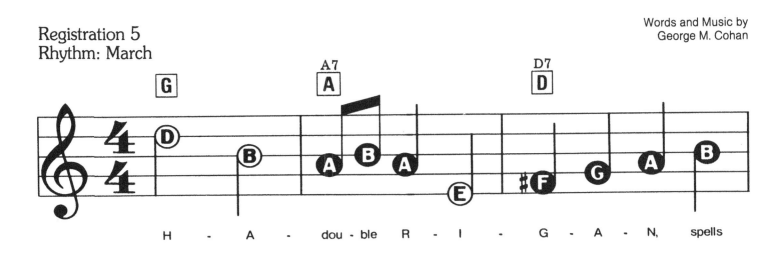

H - A - dou-ble R - I - G - A - N, spells

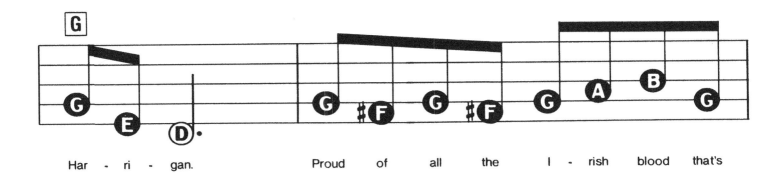

Har - ri - gan.   Proud of all the I - rish blood that's

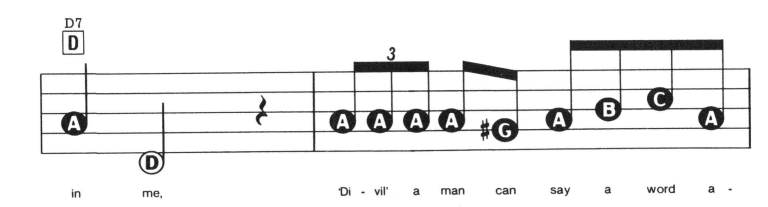

in   me,   'Di - vil' a man can say a word a -

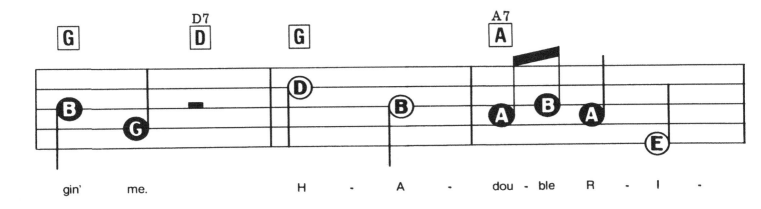

gin' me.   H - A - dou-ble R - I -

13

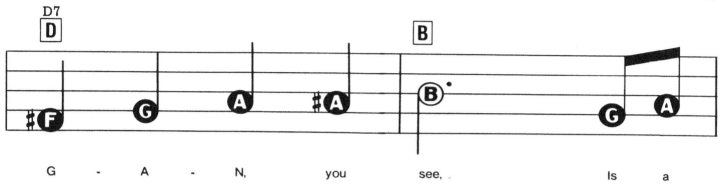

G - A - N, you see, Is a

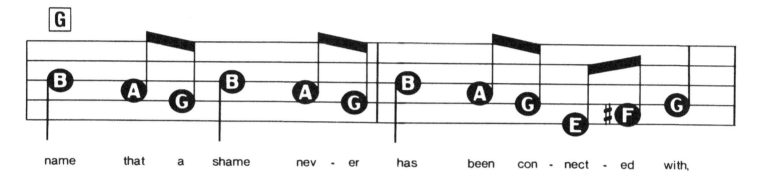

name that a shame nev - er has been con - nect - ed with,

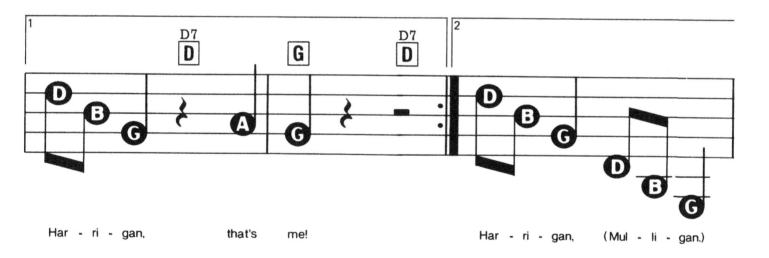

Har - ri - gan, that's me!   Har - ri - gan, (Mul - li - gan.)

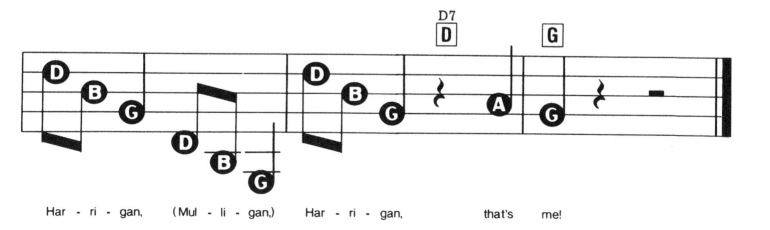

Har - ri - gan, (Mul - li - gan,) Har - ri - gan, that's me!

Has Anybody Here Seen Kelly?

Registration 9
Rhythm: Swing

Words and Music by C.W. Murphy
and Will Letters

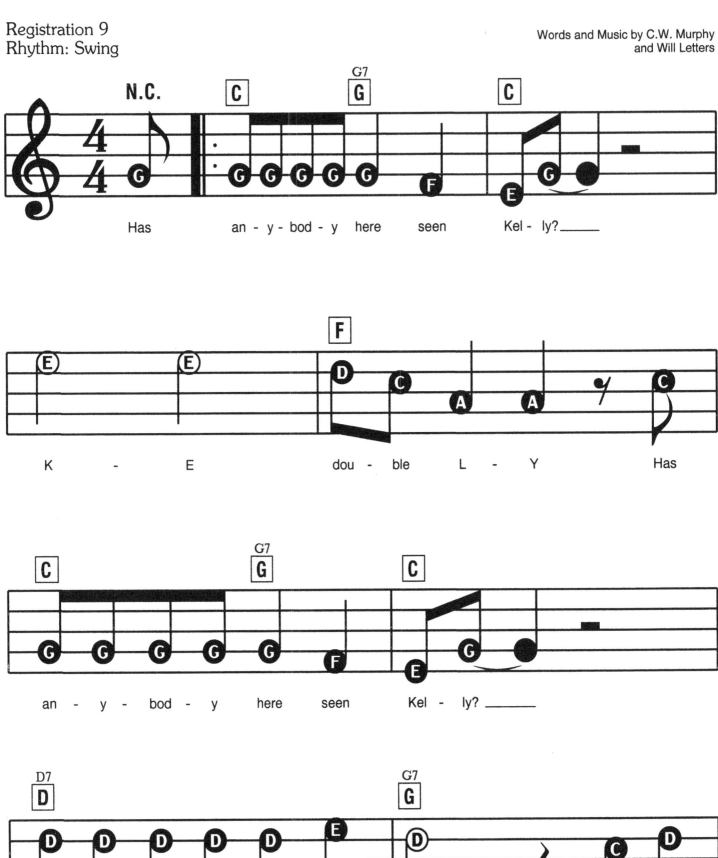

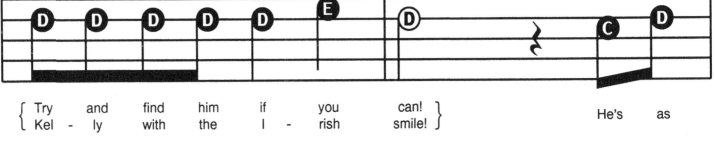

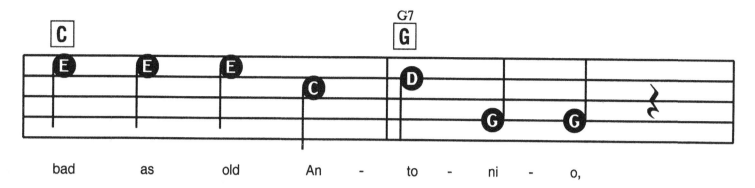

bad   as   old   An -   to -   ni -   o,

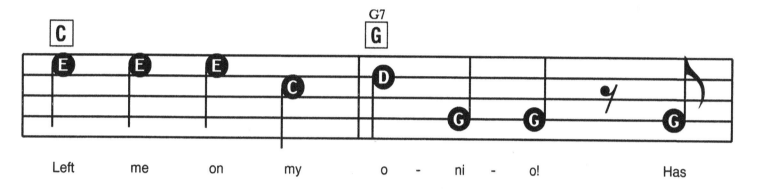

Left   me   on   my   o -   ni -   o!   Has

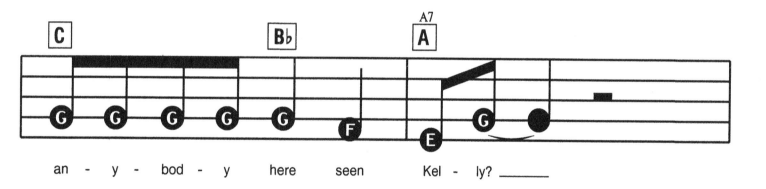

an - y - bod - y   here   seen   Kel - ly? _____

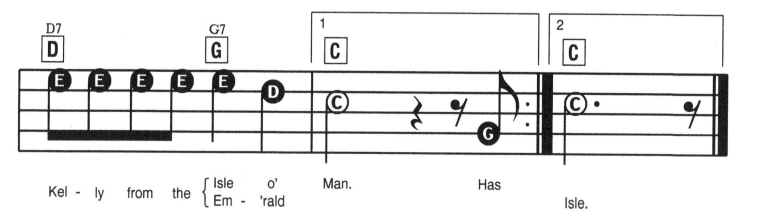

Kel - ly   from   the { Isle o'   Man.   Has
                                { Em - 'rald   Isle.

If I Knock The "L" Out Of Kelly
(It Would Still Be Kelly To Me)

Registration 8
Rhythm: Waltz

Words by Sam M. Lewis and Joe Young
Music by Bert Grant

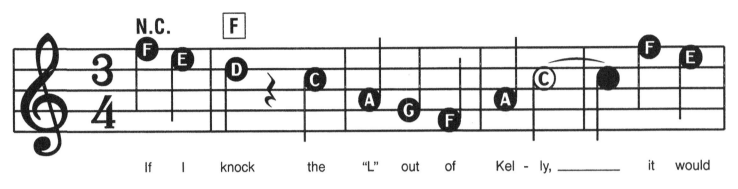

If I knock the "L" out of Kel - ly, _____ it would

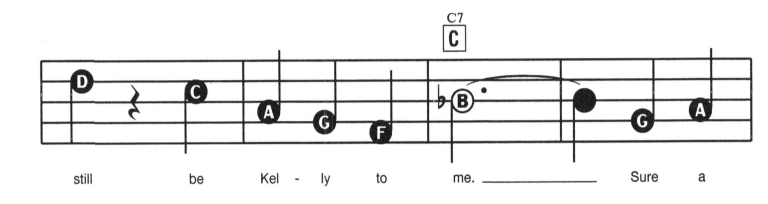

still be Kel - ly to me. _____ Sure a

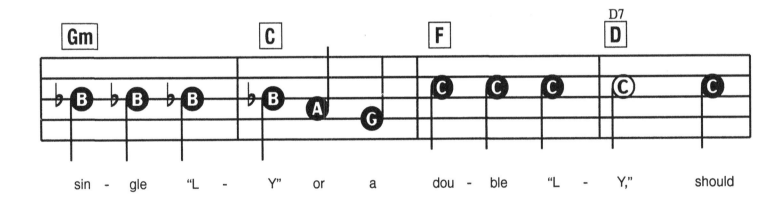

sin - gle "L - Y" or a dou - ble "L - Y," should

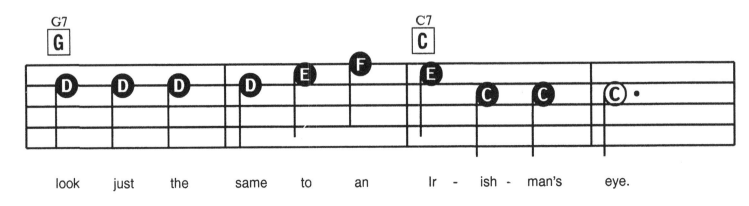

look just the same to an Ir - ish - man's eye.

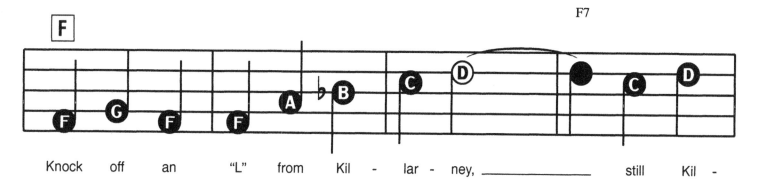

Knock off an "L" from Kil - lar - ney, _____ still Kil -

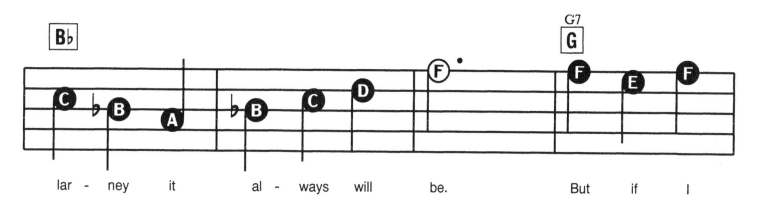

lar - ney it al - ways will be. But if I

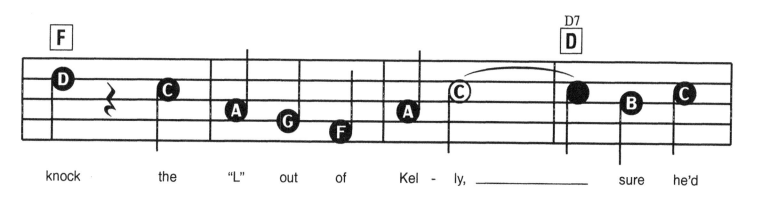

knock the "L" out of Kel - ly, _____ sure he'd

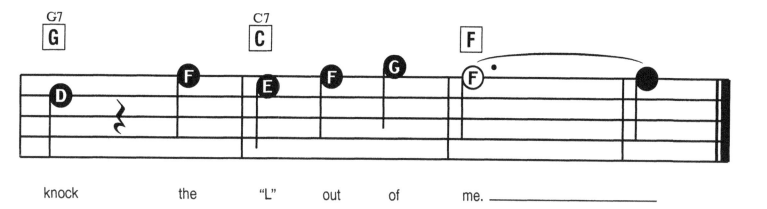

knock the "L" out of me. _____

Irish Washerwoman

Registration 2
Rhythm: Waltz or 6/8 March

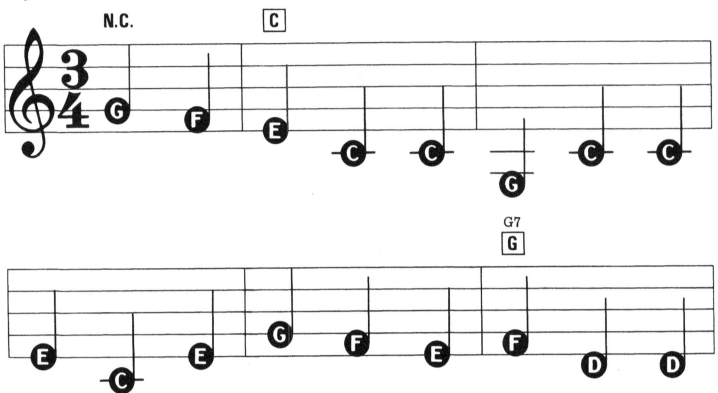

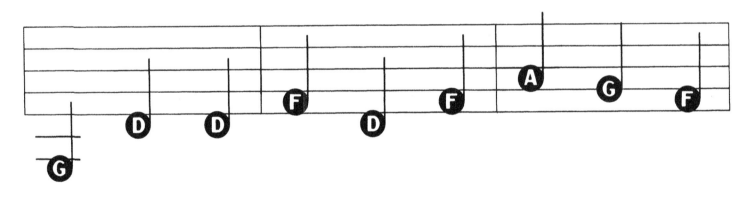

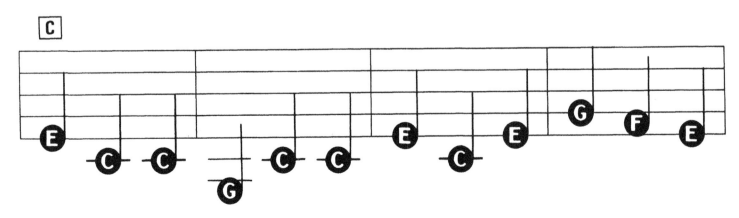

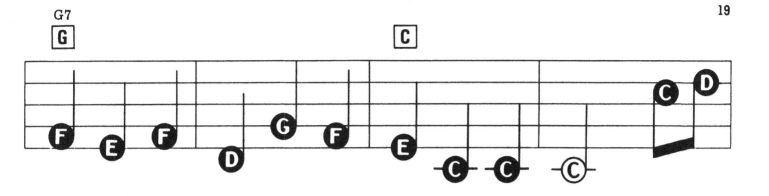

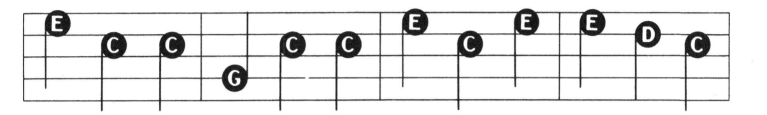

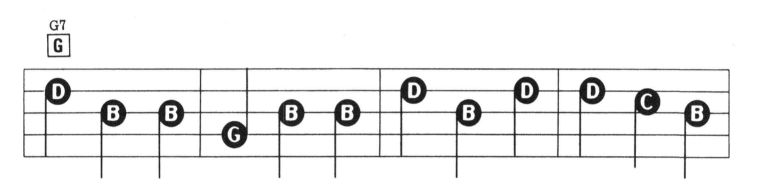

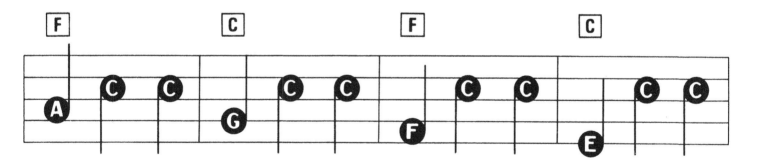

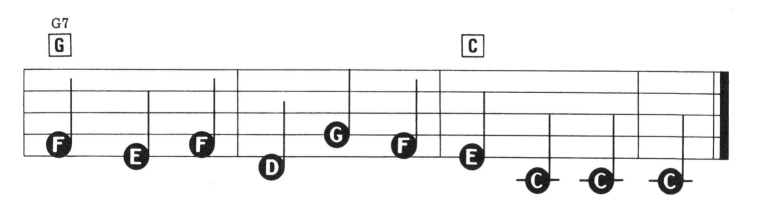

I'll Take You Home Again, Kathleen

Registration 1
Rhythm: Slow Rock or Ballad

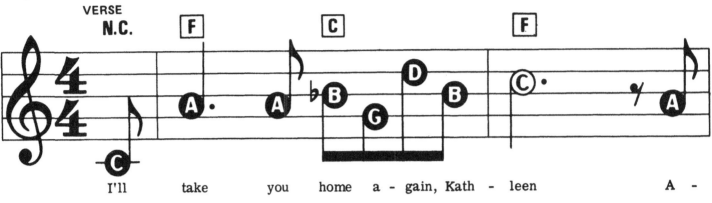

I'll take you home a-gain, Kath-leen A-

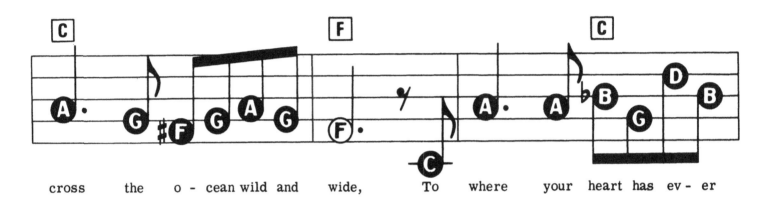

cross the o-cean wild and wide, To where your heart has ev-er

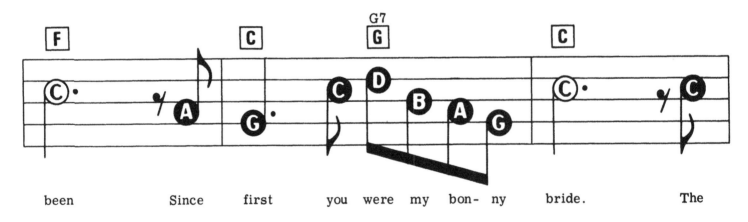

been Since first you were my bon-ny bride. The

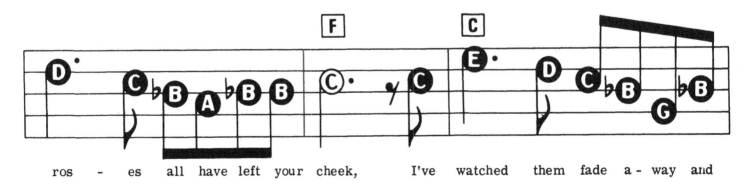

ros - es all have left your cheek, I've watched them fade a-way and

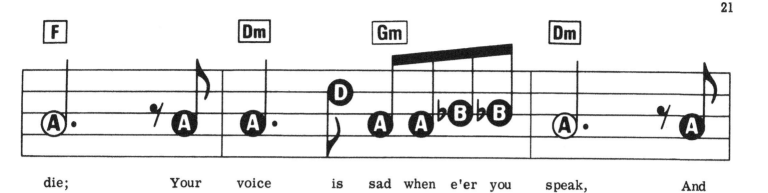

die; Your voice is sad when e'er you speak, And

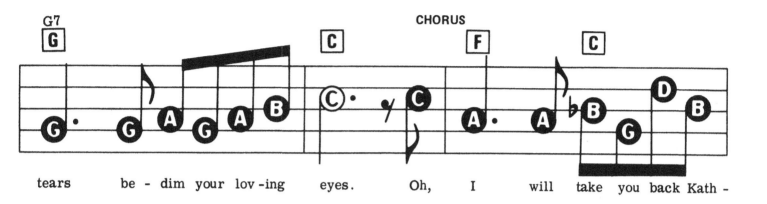

CHORUS

tears be - dim your lov -ing eyes. Oh, I will take you back Kath -

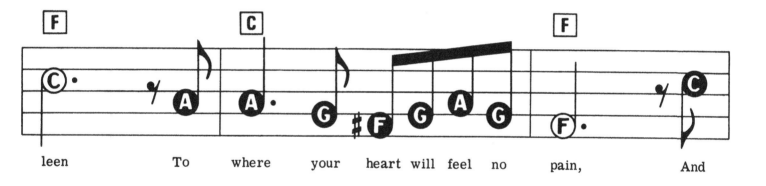

leen To where your heart will feel no pain, And

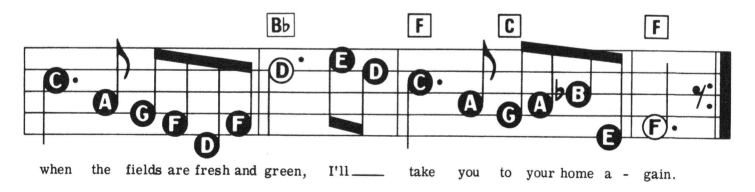

when the fields are fresh and green, I'll____ take you to your home a - gain.

2. I know you love me, Kathleen dear,
 Your heart was ever fond and true,
 I always feel when you are near
 That life holds nothing dear but you.
 The smiles that once you gave to me,
 I scarcely ever see them now,
 Though many, many times I see
 A dark'ning shadow on your brow.
 CHORUS

3. To that dear home beyond the sea
 My Kathleen shall again return,
 And when thy old friends welcome thee,
 Thy loving heart will cease to yearn.
 Where laughs the little silver stream,
 Beside your mother's humble cot,
 And brightest rays of sunshine gleam,
 There all your grief will be forgot.
 CHORUS

Danny Boy
(Londonderry Air)

Registration 10
Rhythm: 8-Beat or Pops

Words by
Frederick E. Weatherly

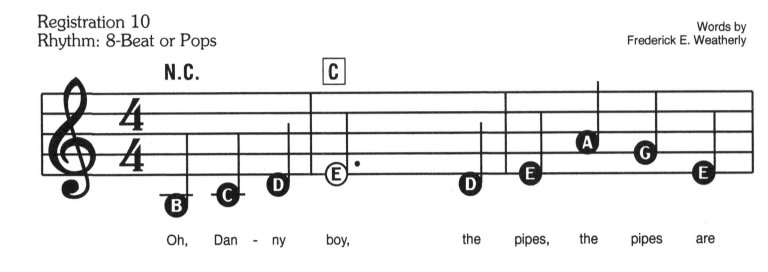

Oh, Dan - ny boy, the pipes, the pipes are

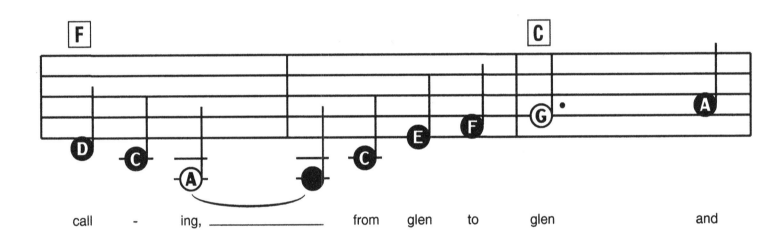

call - ing, _____ from glen to glen and

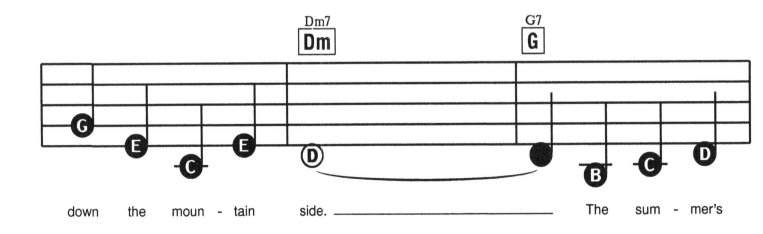

down the moun - tain side. _____ The sum - mer's

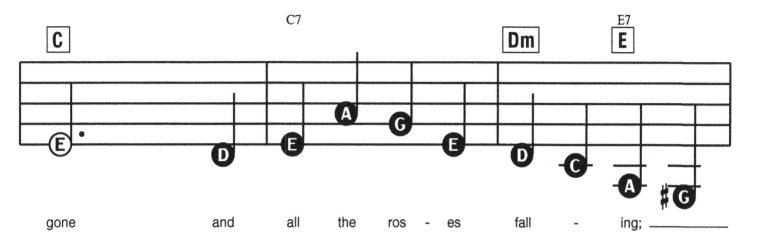

gone   and   all   the   ros - es   fall - ing; _____

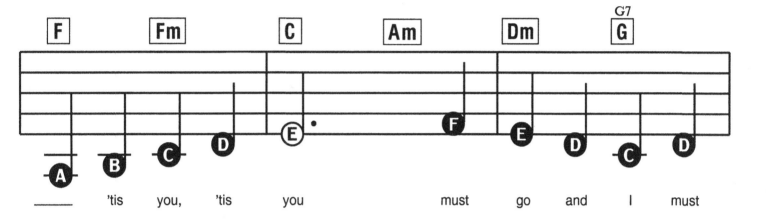

_____ 'tis   you,   'tis   you   must   go   and   I   must

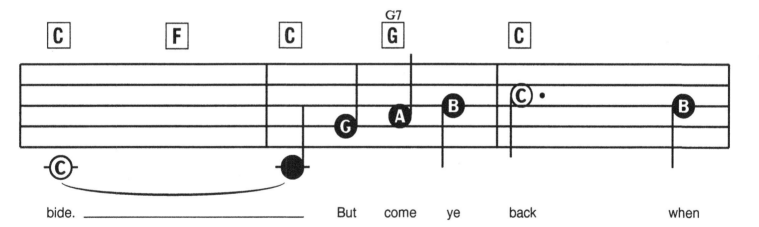

bide. _____ But   come   ye   back   when

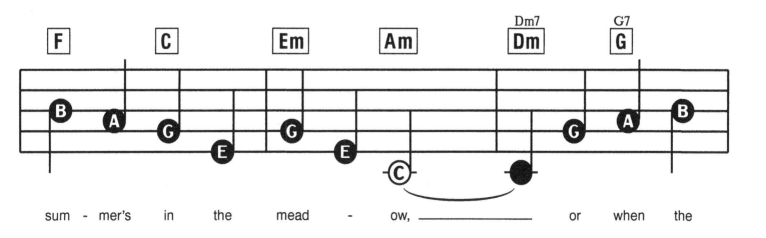

sum - mer's   in   the   mead - ow, _____ or   when   the

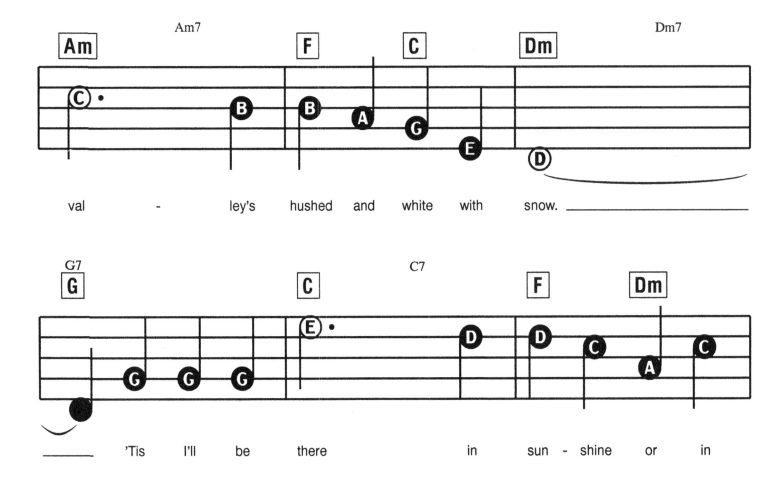

val - ley's hushed and white with snow. _____

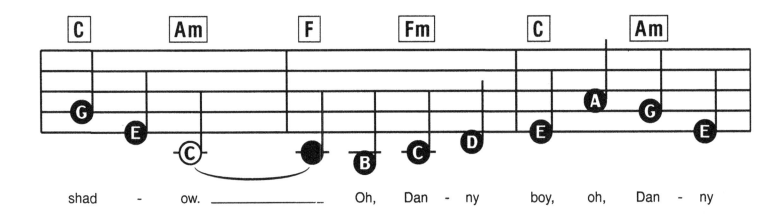

_____ 'Tis I'll be there in sun - shine or in

shad - ow. _____ Oh, Dan - ny boy, oh, Dan - ny

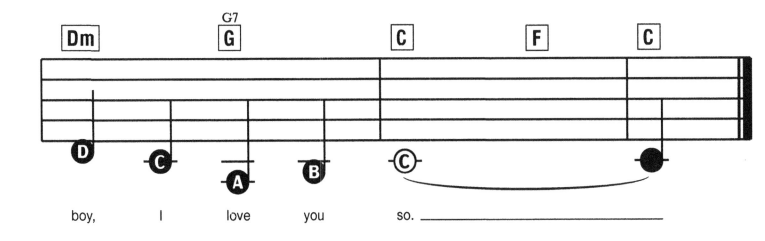

boy, I love you so. _____

Kathleen Mavourneen

Registration 3
Rhythm: Waltz

Kath - leen Ma - vour - neen, the grey dawn is break - ing, The horn of the hunt - er is _____ heard _____ on the hill; The lark from her light wing the bright _____ dew is shak - ing, My _____ Kath - leen Ma - vour - neen, what

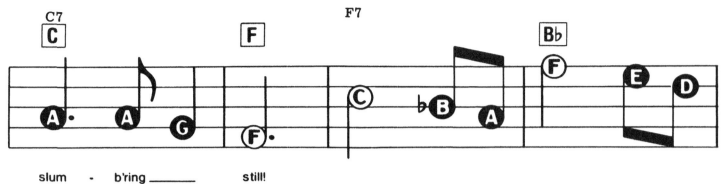

slum - b'ring _____ still!

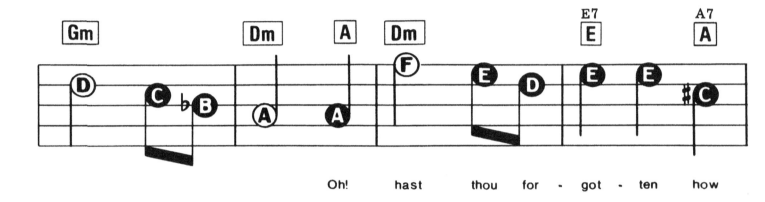

Oh! hast thou for - got - ten how

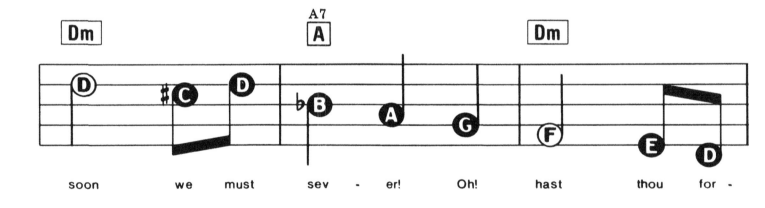

soon we must sev - er! Oh! hast thou for -

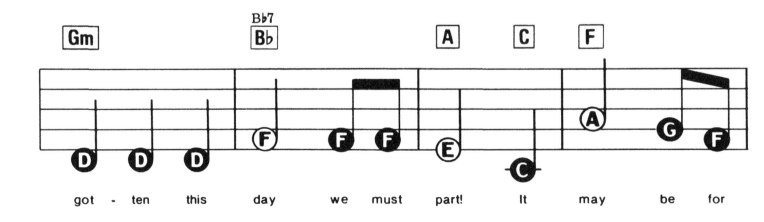

got - ten this day we must part! It may be for

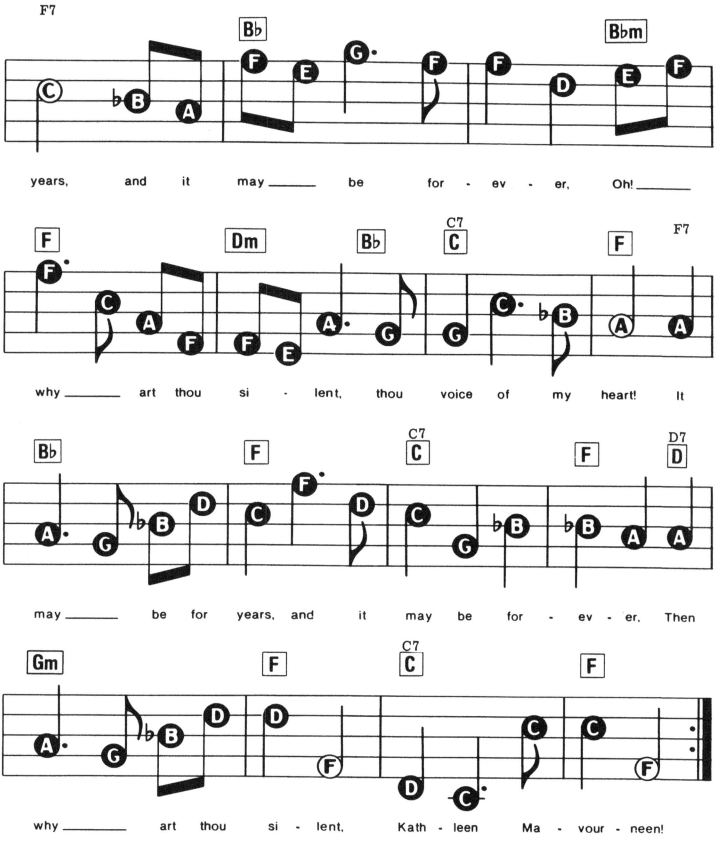

2. Kathleen Mavourneen, awake from thy slumbers
The blue mountains glow in the sun's golden light.
Ah! where is the spell that once hung on thy numbers,
Arise in thy beauty, thou star of my night.
Mauvourneen, Mavourneen, my sad tears are falling,
To think that from Erin and thee I must part,
It may be for years, and it may be for ever,
Then why art thou silent, thou voice of my heart!
It may be for years, and it may be for ever,
Then why art thou silent, Kathleen Mavourneen!

The Kerry Dance

Registration 2
Rhythm: Waltz

O the days of the Ker - ry danc - ing,

O the ring of the pi - per's tune; O for one of those

hours of glad - ness, gone a - las, like our youth too soon.

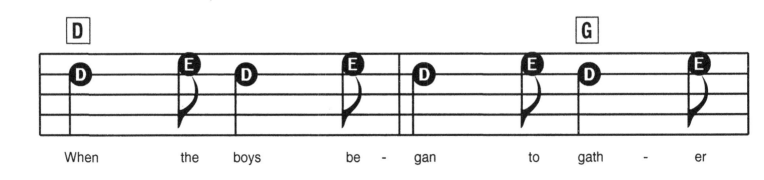

When the boys be - gan to gath - er

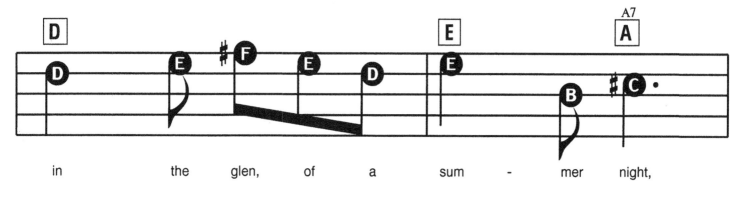

in the glen, of a sum - mer night,

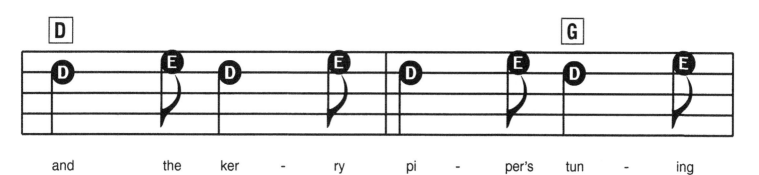

and the ker - ry pi - per's tun - ing

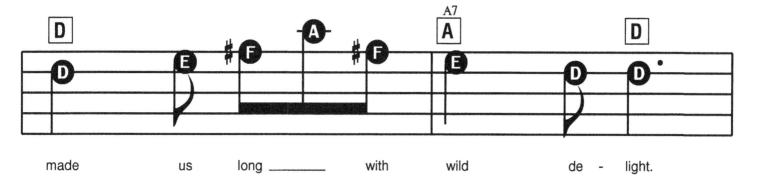

made us long _____ with wild de - light.

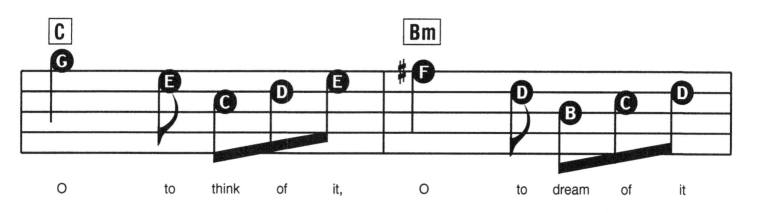

O to think of it, O to dream of it

D.C. al Fine
(Return to beginning
Play to Fine)

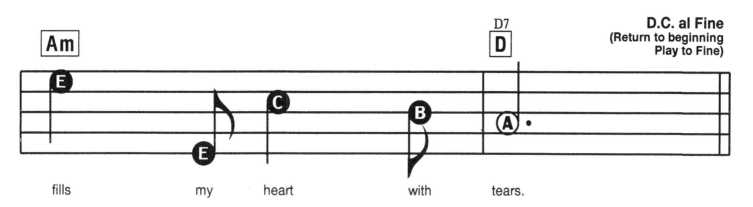

fills my heart with tears.

Killarney

Registration 5
Rhythm: March or Polka

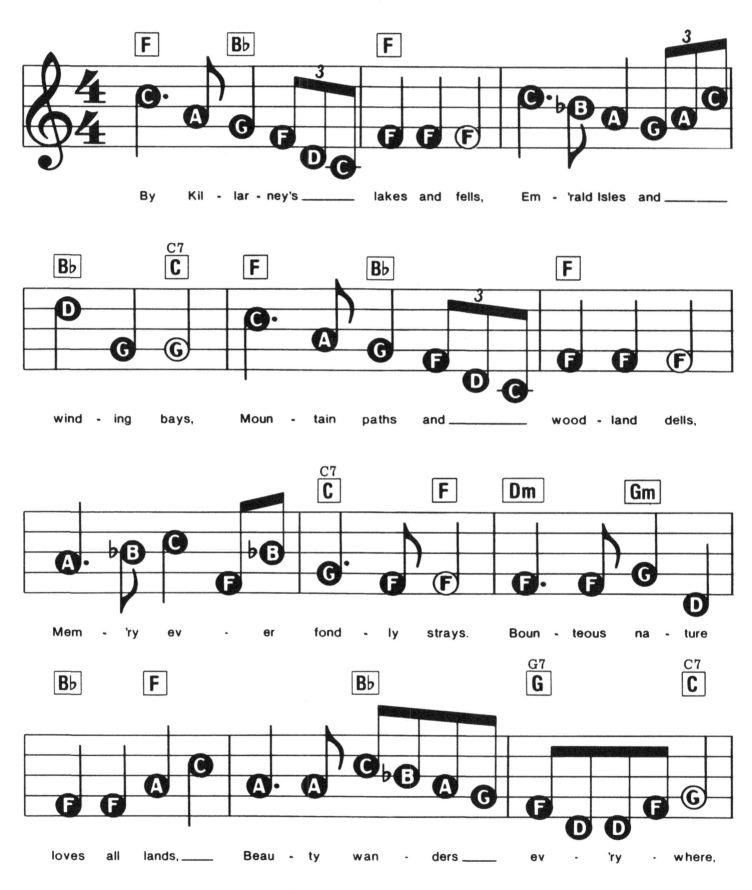

By Kil - lar - ney's _____ lakes and fells, Em - 'rald Isles and _____

wind - ing bays, Moun - tain paths and _____ wood - land dells,

Mem - 'ry ev - er fond - ly strays. Boun - teous na - ture

loves all lands, _____ Beau - ty wan - ders _____ ev - 'ry - where,

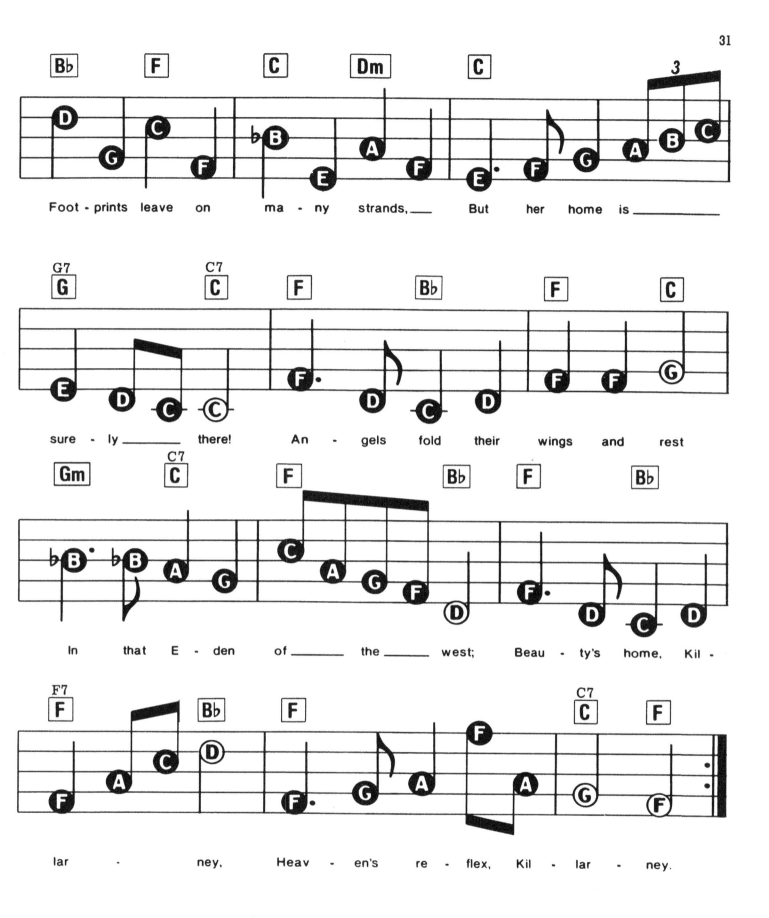

2. No place else can charm the eye
   With such bright and varied tints,
   Ev'ry rock that you pass by
   Verdure broiders or besprints.
   Virgin there the green grass grows,
   Ev'ry morn Spring's natal day,
   Bright hued berries daff the snows,
   Smiling Winter's frown away.
   Angels often pausing there
   Doubt if Eden were more fair;
   Beauty's home, Killarney.
   Heaven's reflex, Killarney.

Kitty Of Coleraine

Registration 7
Rhythm: Waltz

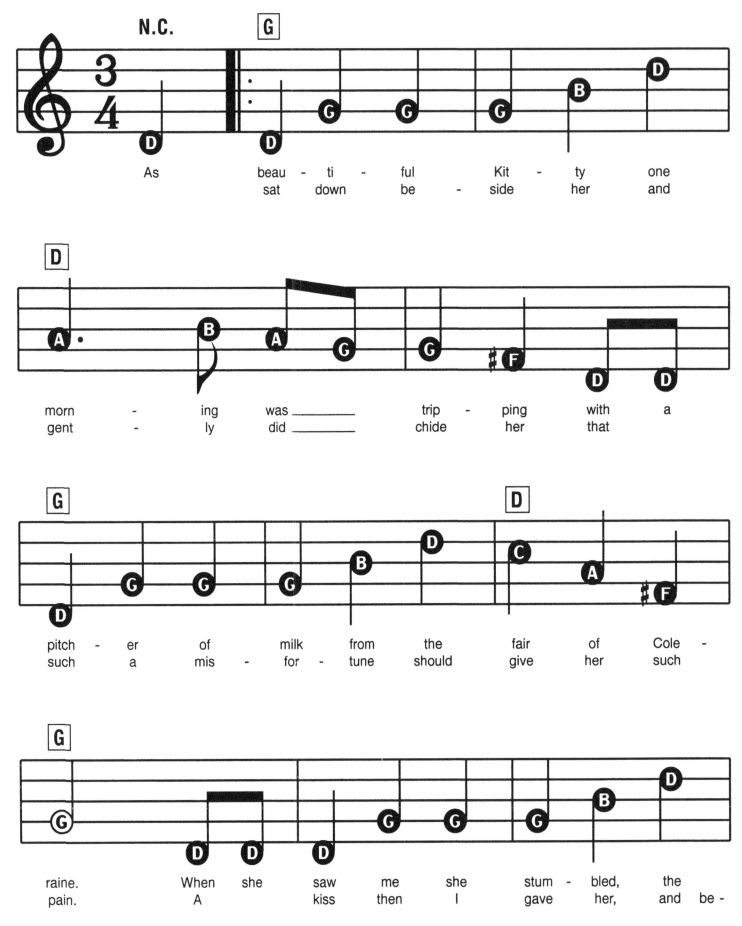

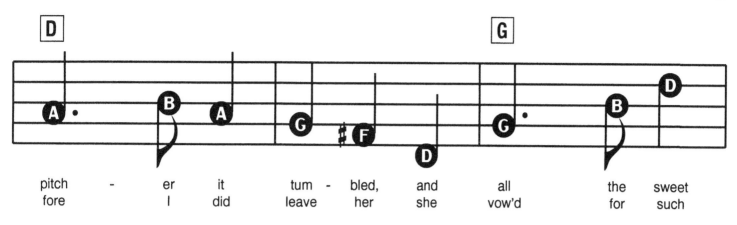

pitch - er it tum - bled, and all the sweet
fore I did leave her and she vow'd for such

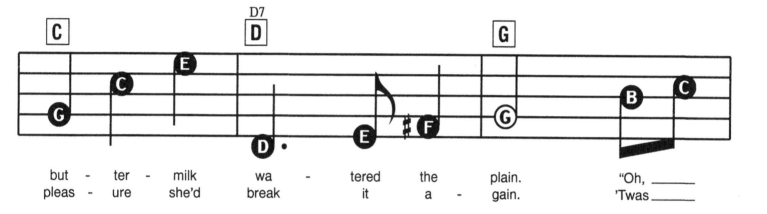

but - ter - milk wa - tered the plain. "Oh, _____
pleas - ure she'd break it a - gain. 'Twas _____

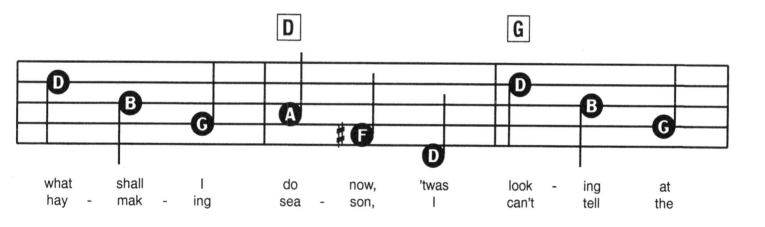

what shall I do now, 'twas look - ing at
hay - mak - ing sea - son, I can't tell the

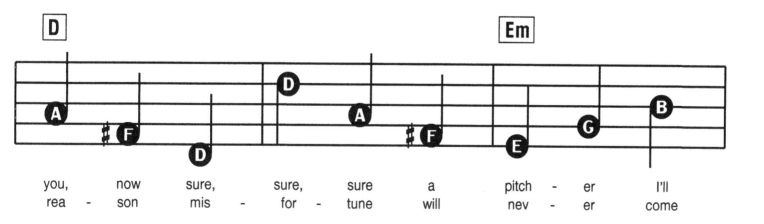

you, now sure, sure, sure a pitch - er I'll
rea - son mis - for - tune will nev - er come

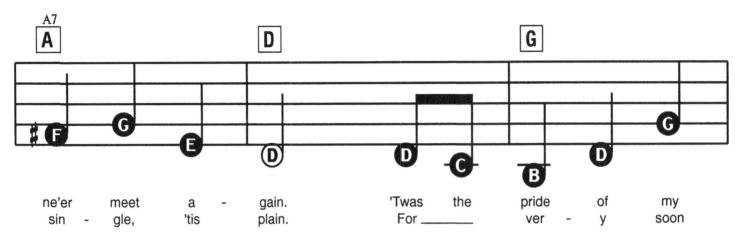

ne'er meet a - gain. 'Twas the pride of my
sin - gle, 'tis plain. For _____ ver - y soon

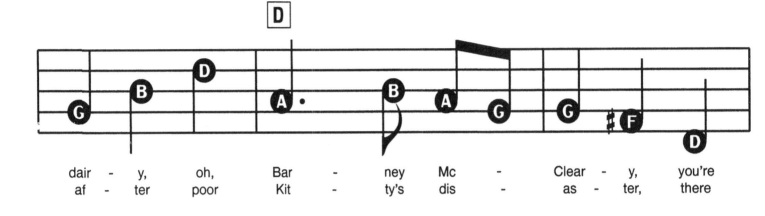

dair - y, oh, Bar - ney Mc - Clear - y, you're
af - ter poor Kit - ty's dis - as - ter, there

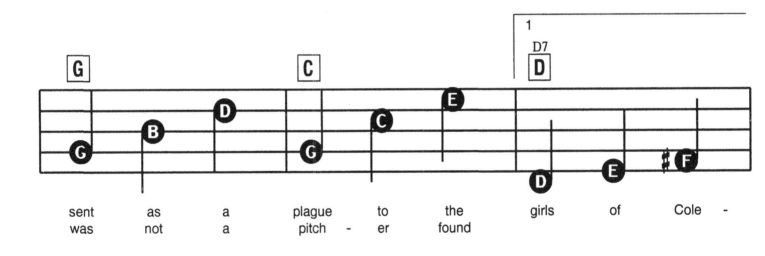

sent as a plague to the girls of Cole -
was not a pitch - er found

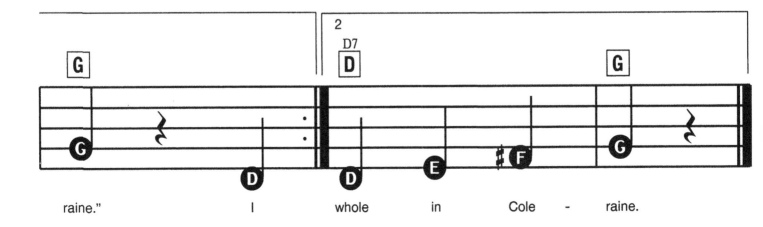

raine." I whole in Cole - raine.

McNamara's Band

Registration 5
Rhythm: 6/8 March

Words by John J. Stamford
Music by Shamus O'Conner

N.C.

F

Oh! me name is Mc - Na - mar - a, I'm the
now we are re - hear - sin' for a

lead - er of the band, ———— al -
ver - y swell af - fair, ———— the

C7
C

F

Dm

though we're few in num - bers we're the
an - nual cel - e - bra - tion, all the

G7
G

C7
C

F

fin - est in the land. We play at wakes and
gen - try will be there. When Gen - eral Grant and to

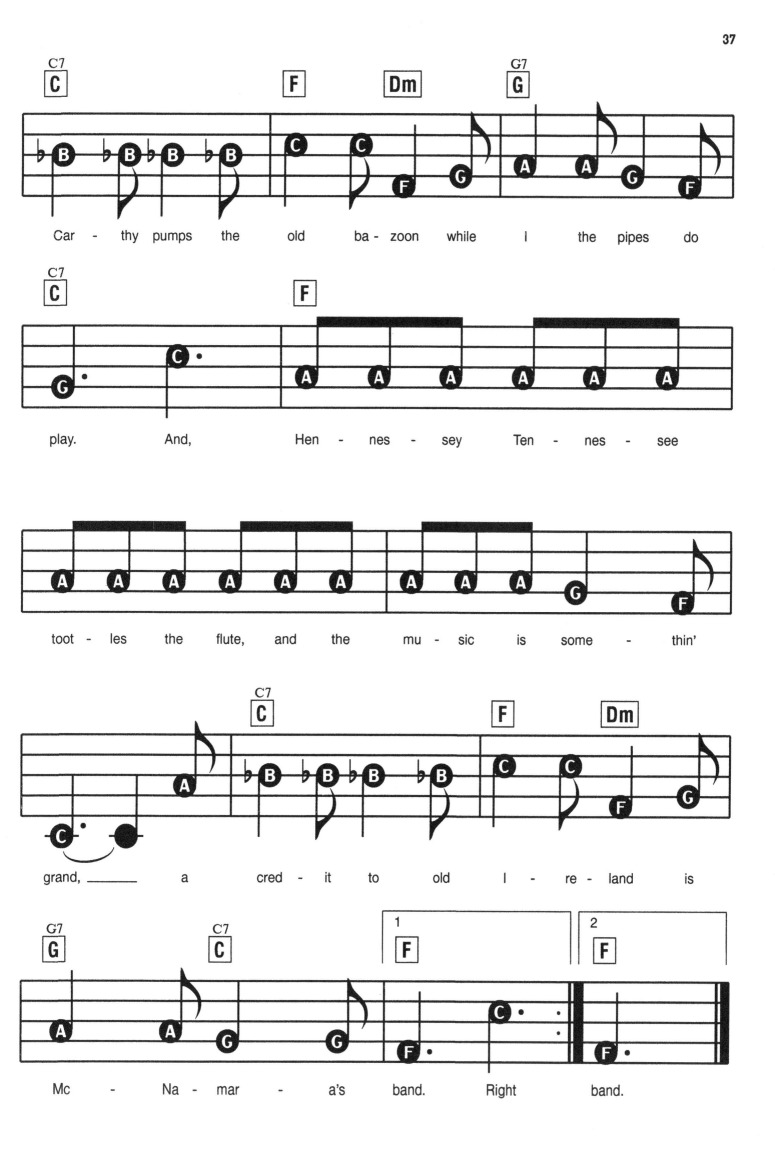

A Little Bit Of Heaven
(Shure They Call It Ireland)

Registration 9
Rhythm: Slow Rock or Ballad

Words by J. Keirn Brenan
Music by Ernest R. Ball

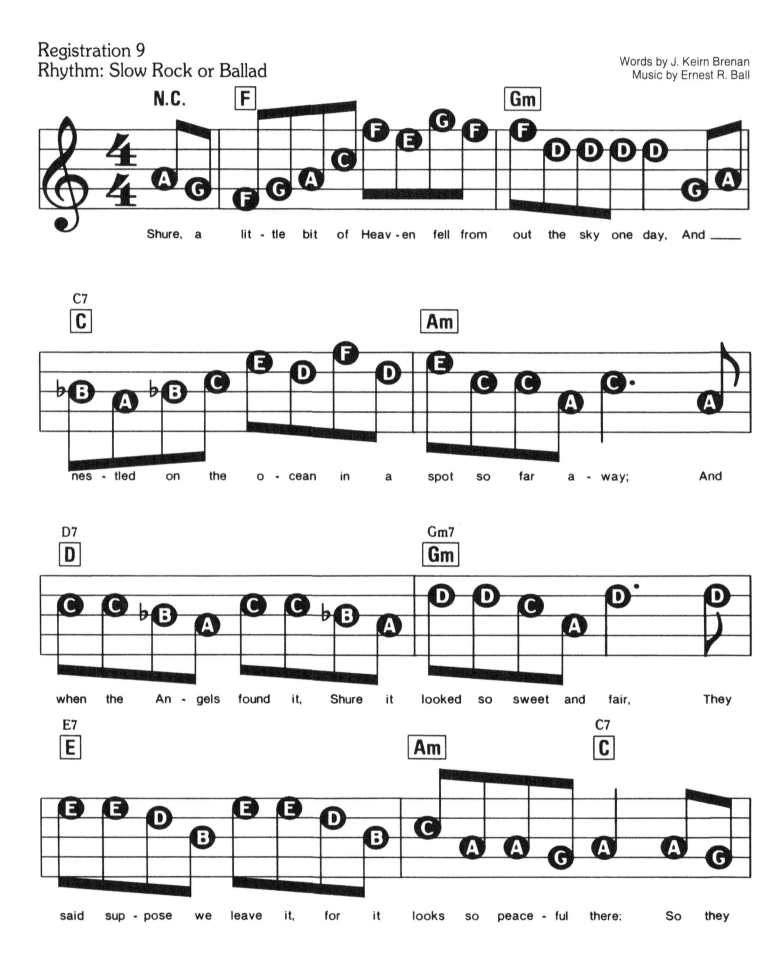

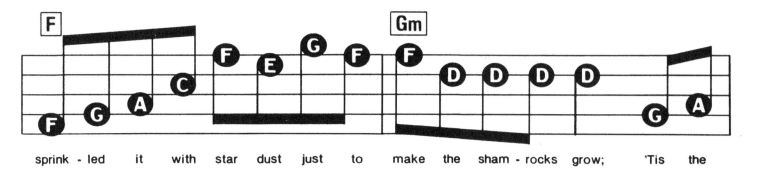

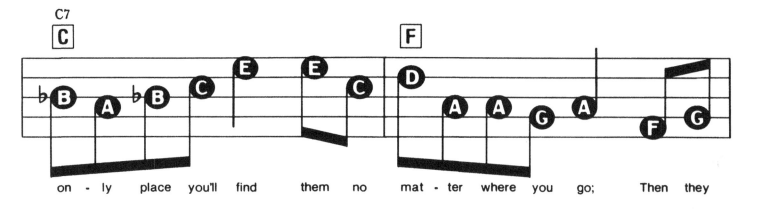

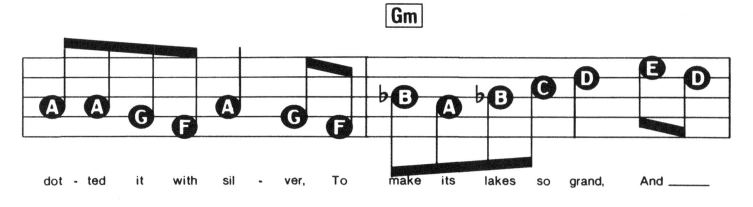

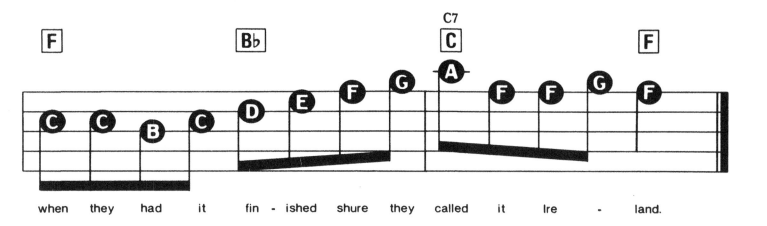

The Minstrel Boy

Registration 3
Rhythm: March

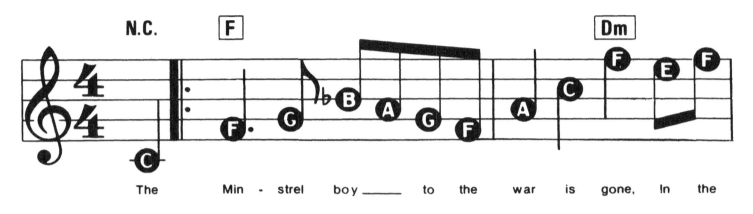

The Min - strel boy ____ to the war is gone, In the

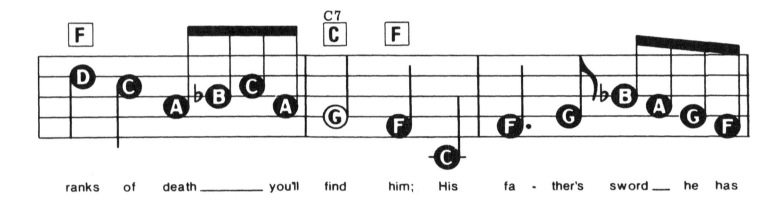

ranks of death ____ you'll find him; His fa - ther's sword ___ he has

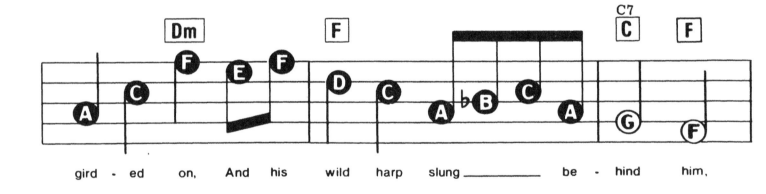

gird - ed on, And his wild harp slung ____ be - hind him,

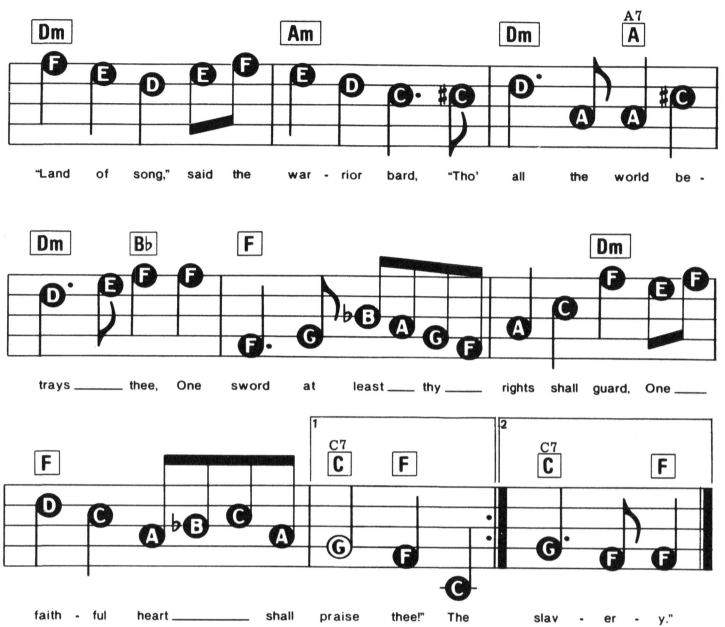

"Land of song," said the war - rior bard, "Tho' all the world be -

trays _____ thee, One sword at least ___ thy _____ rights shall guard, One ____

faith - ful heart _____ shall praise thee!" The slav - er - y."

2. The Minstrel fell,
   But the foe man's chain could not bring his proud soul under;
   The harp he loved ne'er spoke again,
   For he tore its chords asunder,
   And said, "No chain shall sully thee,
   Thou soul of love and bravery!
   Thy songs were made for the pure and free,
   They ne'er shall sound in slavery."

Molly Malone
(Cockles And Mussels)

Registration 1
Rhythm: Waltz

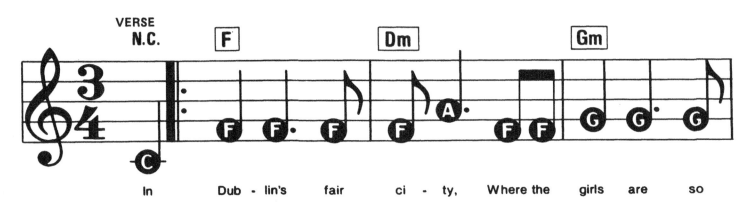

In Dub - lin's fair ci - ty, Where the girls are so

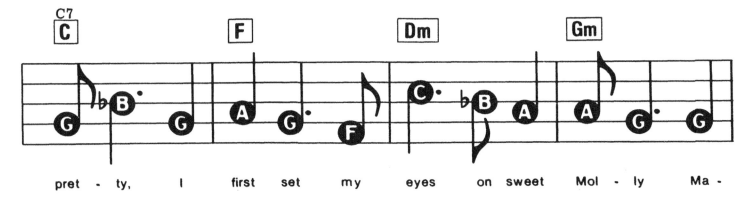

pret - ty, I first set my eyes on sweet Mol - ly Ma -

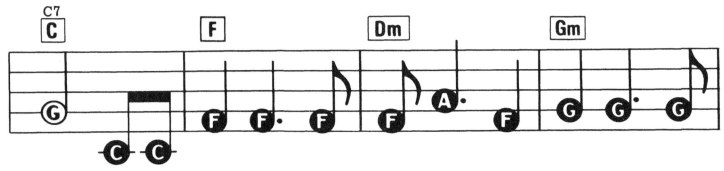

lone, As she wheel'd her wheel - bar - row Through streets broad and

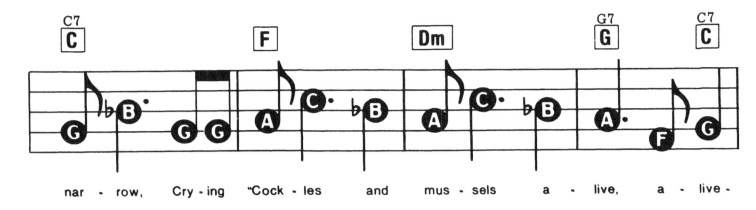

nar - row, Cry - ing "Cock - les and mus - sels a - live, a - live -

CHORUS

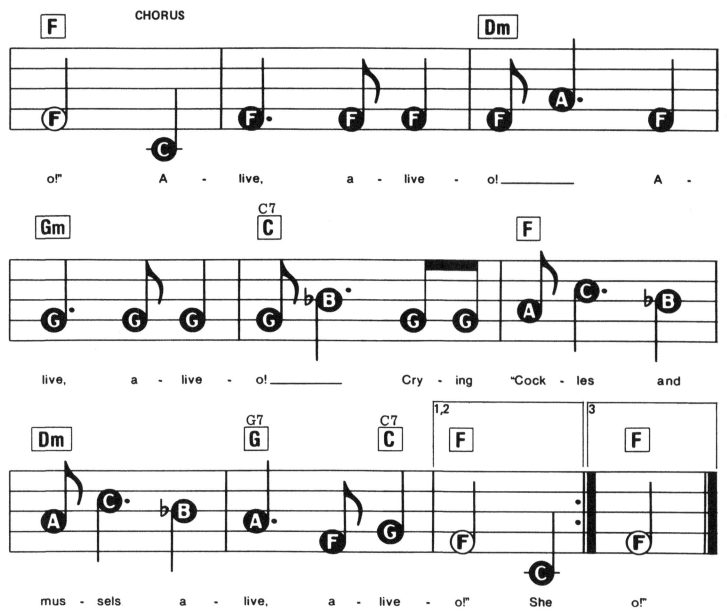

2. She was a fishmonger, But sure 'twas no wonder,
For so were her father and mother before,
And they each wheel'd their barrow,
Through streets broad and narrow,
Crying "Cockles and mussels alive, alive-o!"
CHORUS

3. She died of a fever, And no one could save her,
And that was the end of sweet Molly Malone,
But her ghost wheels her barrow
Through streets broad and narrow,
Crying "Cockles and mussels alive, alive-o!"
CHORUS

My Wild Irish Rose

Registration 2
Rhythm: Waltz

Words and Music by
Chauncey Olcott

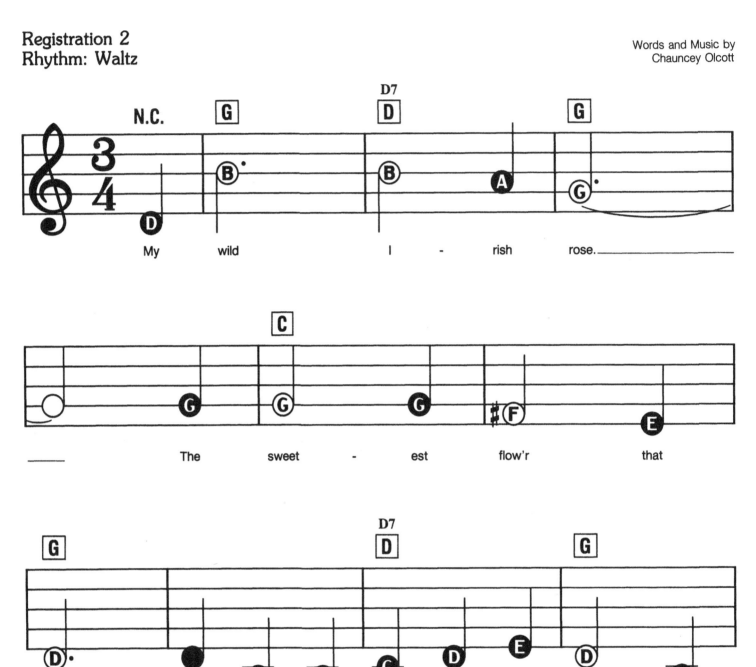

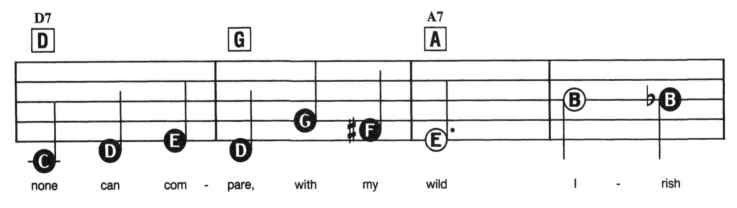

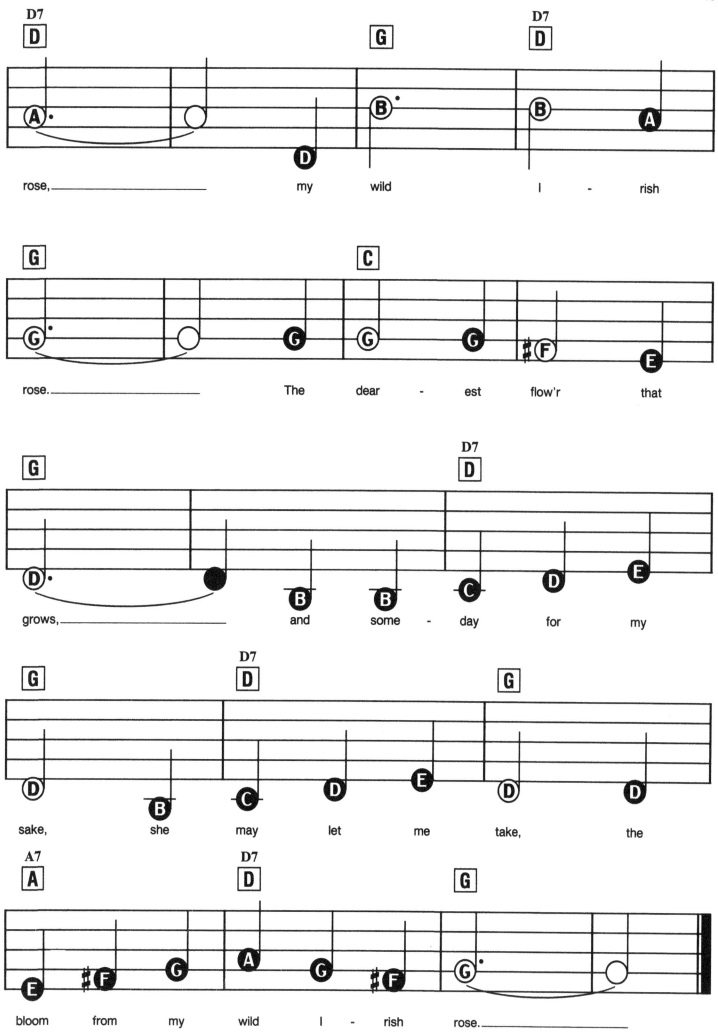

Mother Machree

Registration 2
Rhythm: Waltz

Words by Rita Johnson Young
Music by Ernest R. Ball and Chauncey Olcott

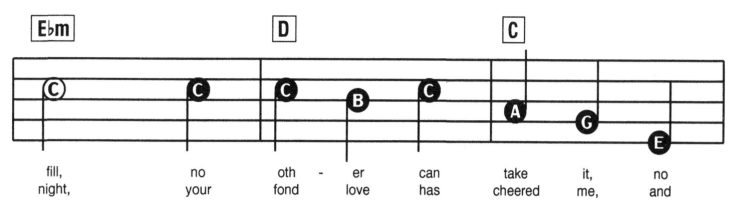

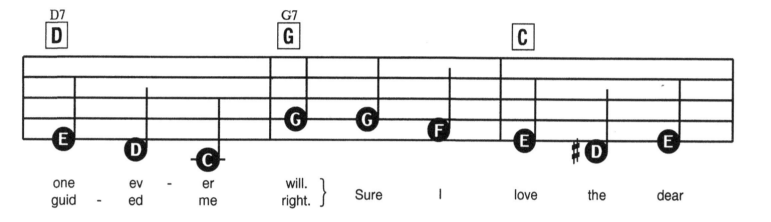

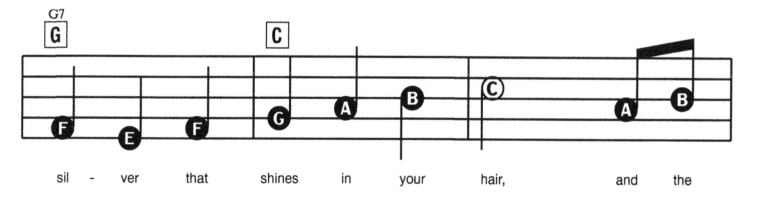

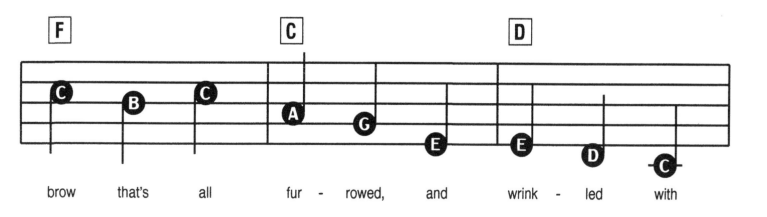

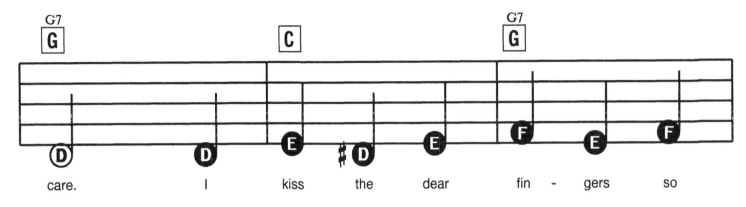

care. I kiss the dear fin - gers so

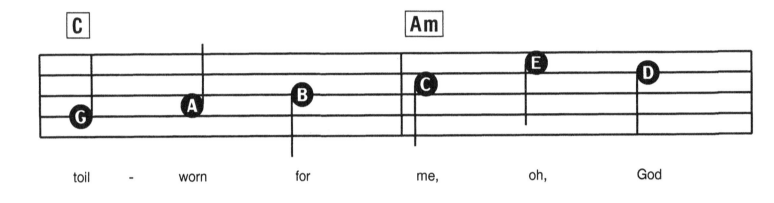

toil - worn for me, oh, God

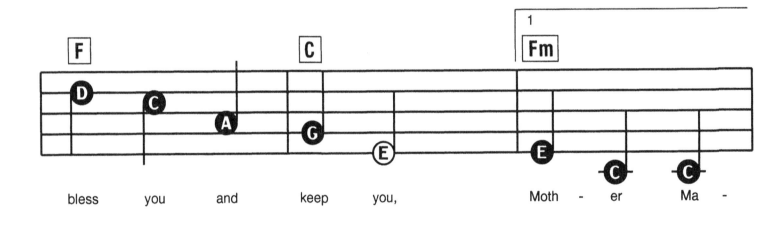

bless you and keep you, Moth - er Ma -

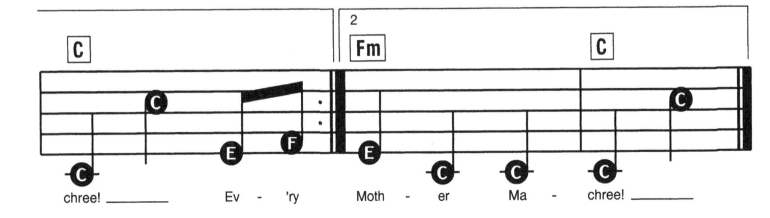

chree! _____ Ev - 'ry Moth - er Ma - chree! _____

Rory O'Moore

Registration 9
Rhythm: 6/8 March

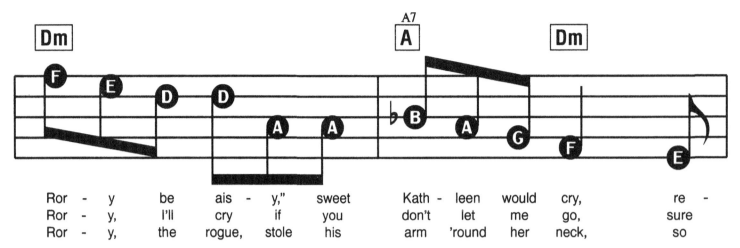

Ror - y be ais - y," sweet Kath - leen would cry, re -
Ror - y, I'll cry if you don't let me go, sure
Ror - y, the rogue, stole his arm 'round her neck, so

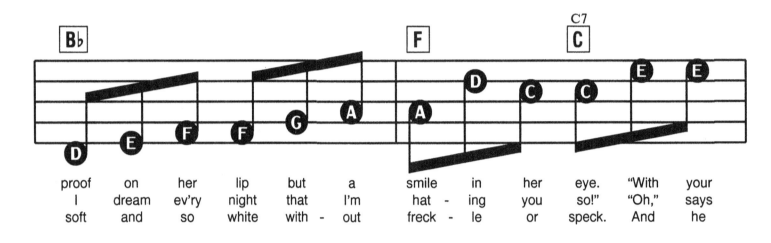

proof on her lip but a smile in her eye. "With your
I dream ev'ry night that I'm hat - ing you so!" "Oh," says
soft and so white with - out freck - le or speck. And he

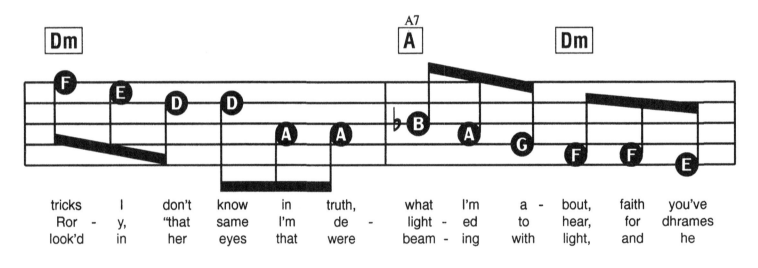

tricks I don't know in truth, what I'm a - bout, faith you've
Ror - y, "that same I'm de - light - ed to hear, for dhrames
look'd in her eyes that were beam - ing with light, and he

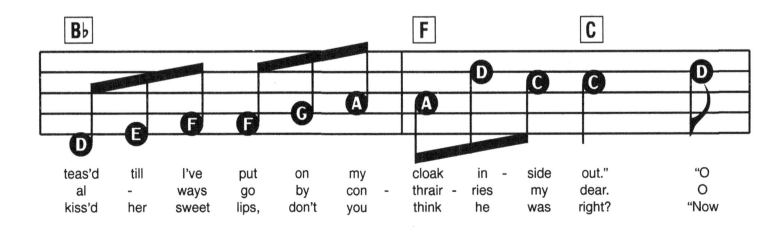

teas'd till I've put on my cloak in - side out." "O
al - ways go by my con - thrair - ries my dear. O
kiss'd her sweet lips, don't you think he was right? "Now

The Rose Of Tralee

Registration 3
Rhythm: Waltz

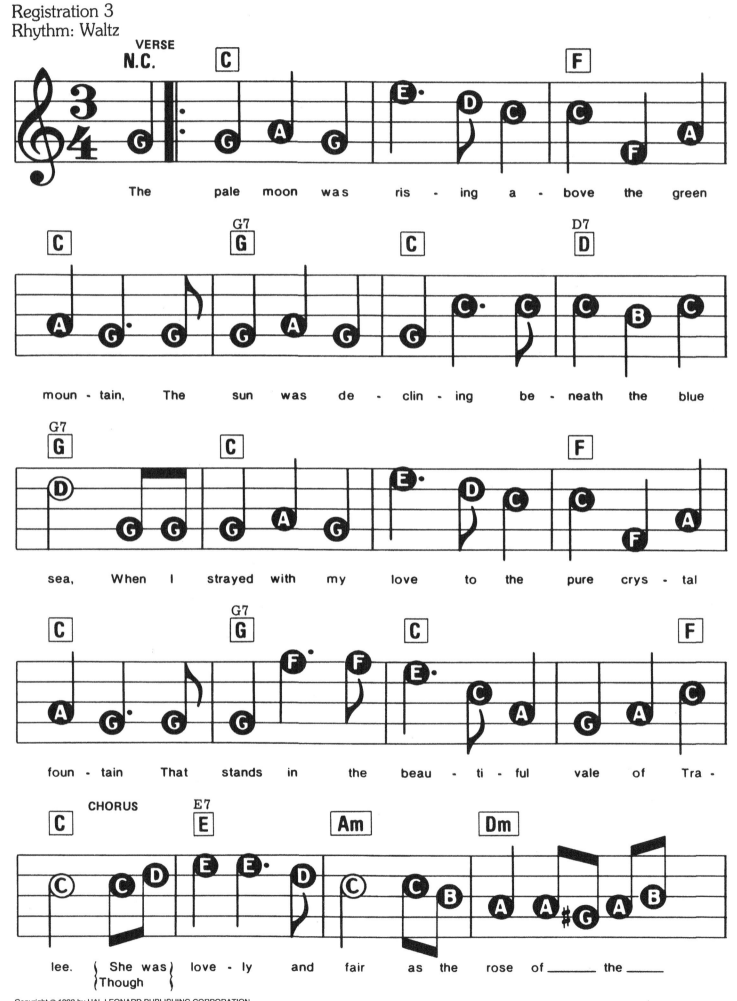

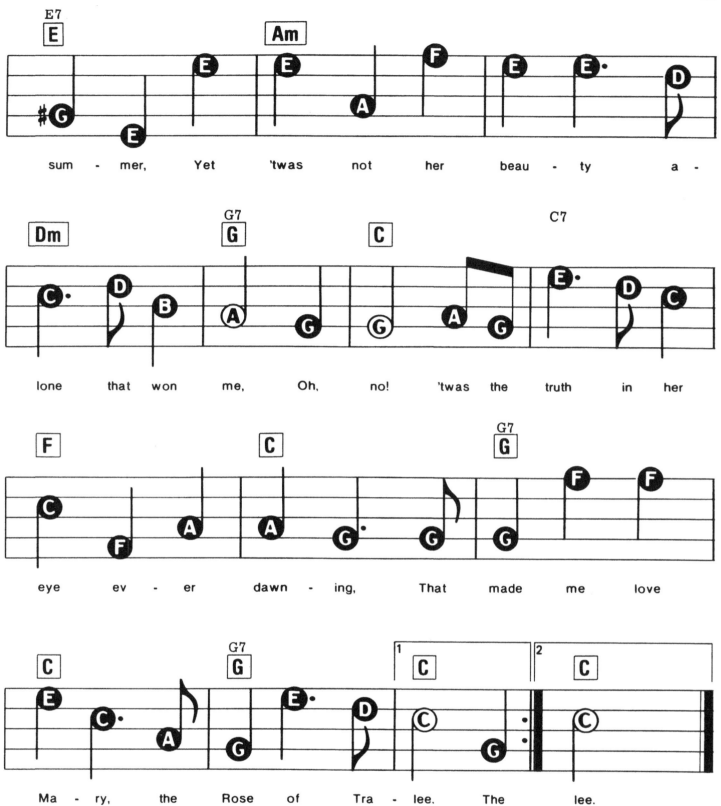

2. The cool shades of ev'ning their mantle were spreading,
   And Mary all smiling was list'ning to me,
   The moon through the valley her pale rays was shedding,
   When I won the heart of the Rose of Tralee.
   CHORUS

Sweet Rosie O'Grady

Registration 4
Rhythm: Waltz

Words and Music by
Maude Nugent

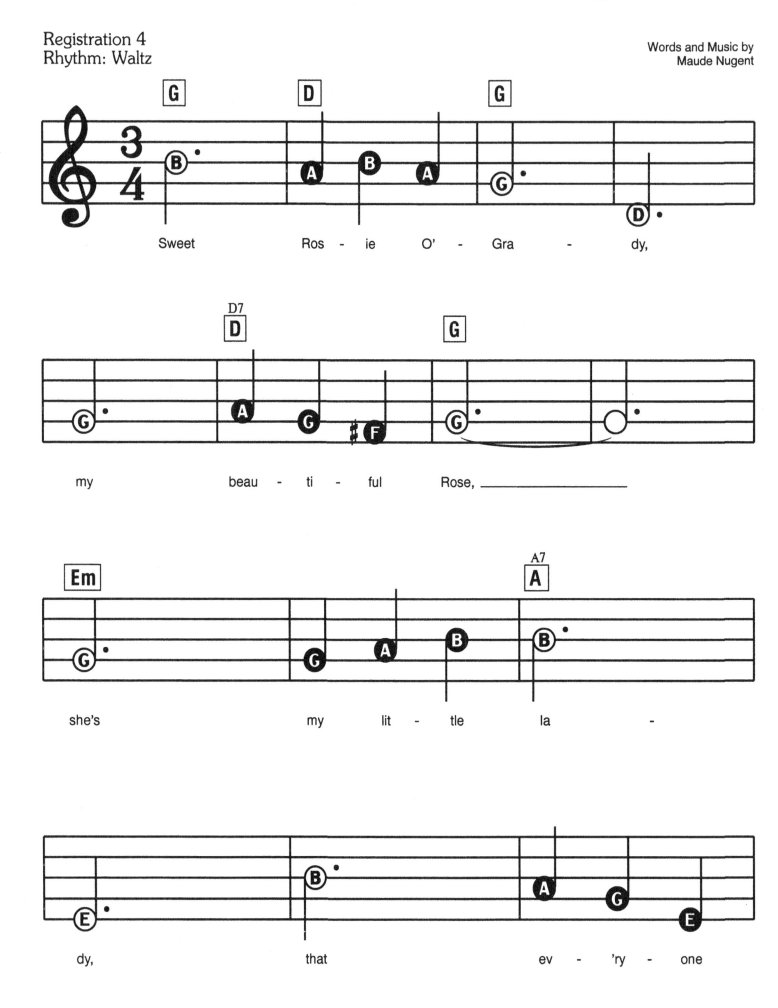

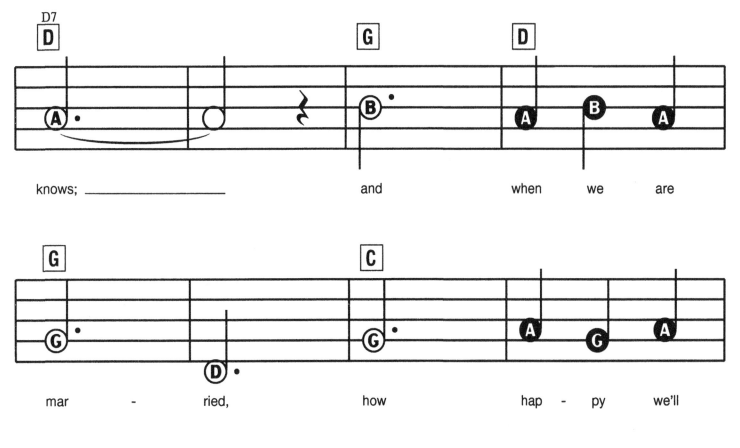

knows; _____ and when we are

mar - ried, how hap - py we'll

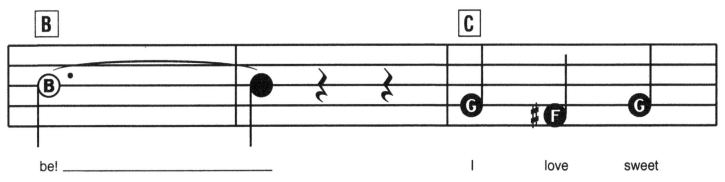

be! _____ I love sweet

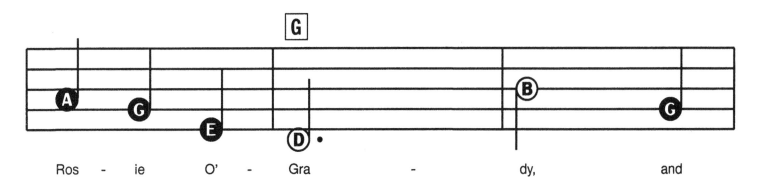

Ros - ie O' - Gra - dy, and

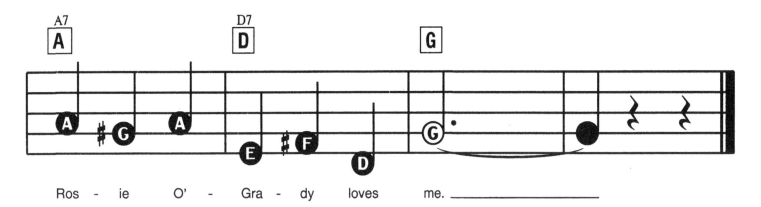

Ros - ie O' - Gra - dy loves me. _____

'Tis The Last Rose Of Summer

Registration 10
Rhythm: Waltz

Words by Thomas Moore
Music by Richard Alfred Milliken

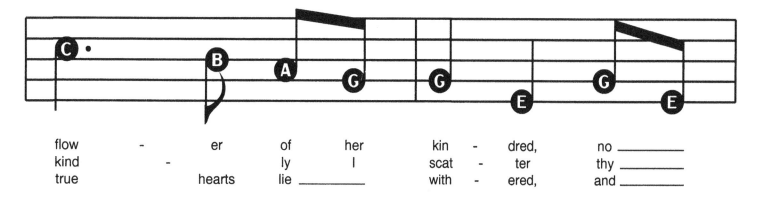

flow - er of her kin - dred, no _____
kind - ly I scat - ter thy _____
true hearts lie _____ with - ered, and _____

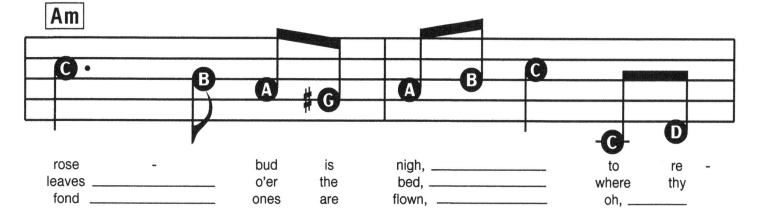

Am

rose - bud is nigh, _____ to re -
leaves _____ o'er the bed, _____ where thy
fond _____ ones are flown, _____ oh, _____

C

flect back _____ her _____ blush - es, or _____
mates of _____ the _____ gar - den lie _____
who would _____ in - hab - it this _____

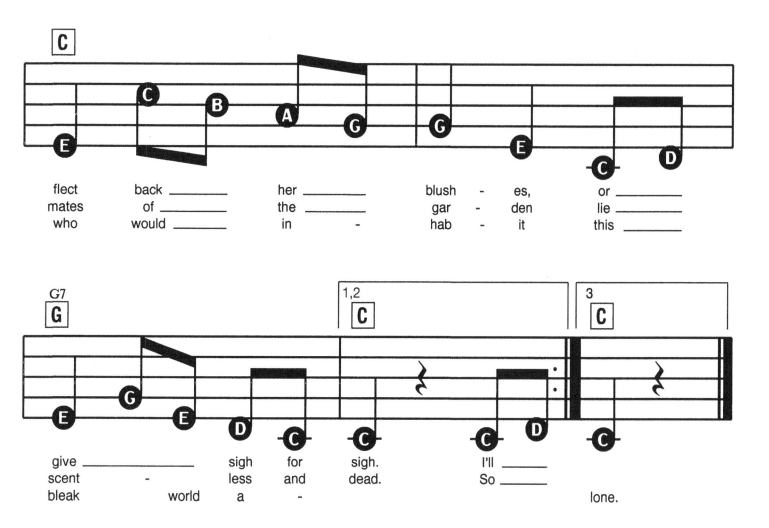

G7
G

1,2
C

3
C

give _____ sigh for sigh. I'll _____
scent - less a - and dead. So _____
bleak world a - lone.

Too-Ra-Loo-Ra-Loo-Ral
(That's An Irish Lullaby)

Registration 1
Rhythm: Waltz

Words and Music by
J.R. Shannon

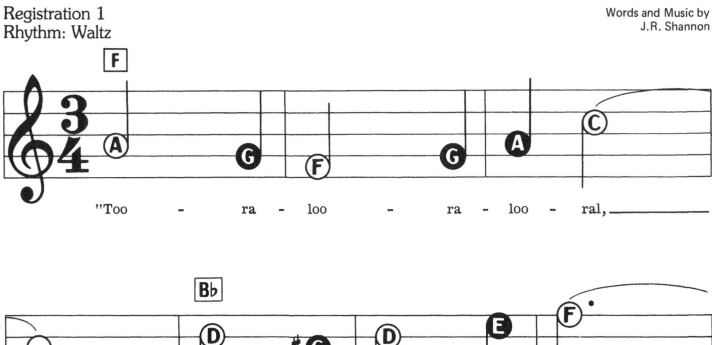

"Too - ra - loo - ra - loo - ral,_____

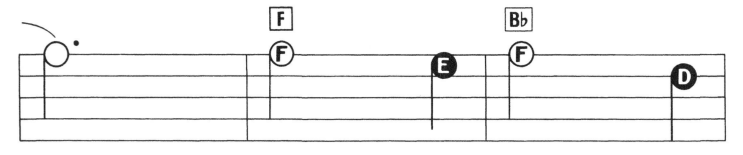

_____ Too - ra - loo - ra - li,_____

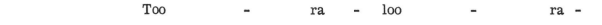

_____ Too - ra - loo - ra -

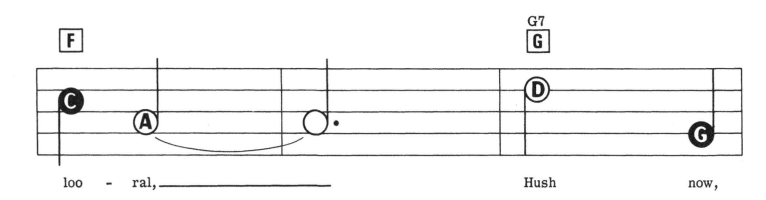

loo - ral,_____ Hush now,

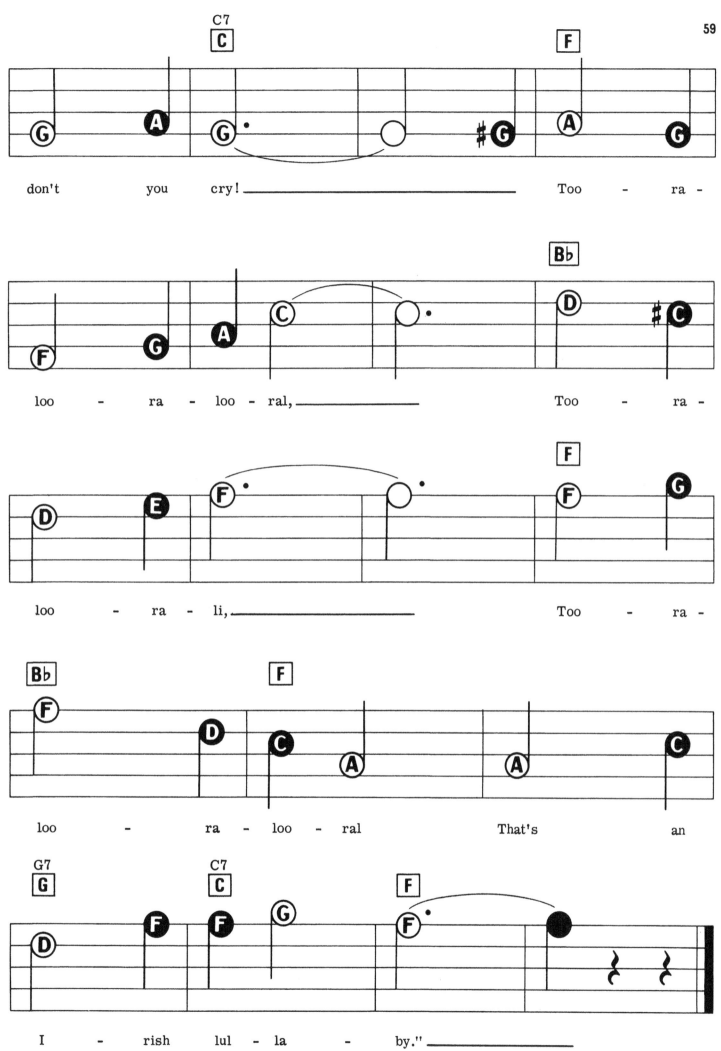

Tourelay

Registration 8
Rhythm: Waltz

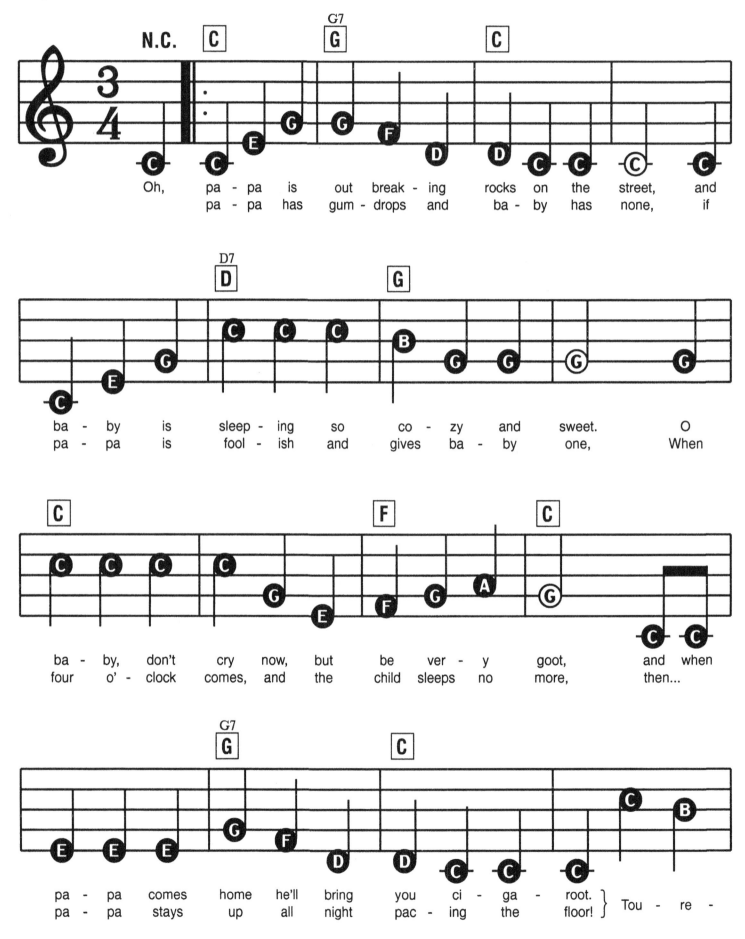

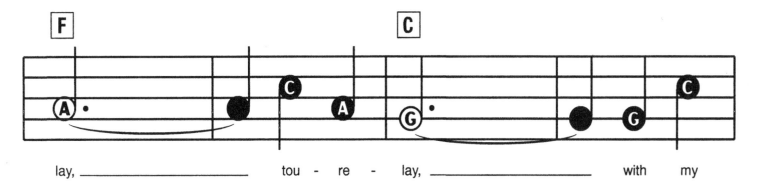

lay, _____ tou - re - lay, _____ with my

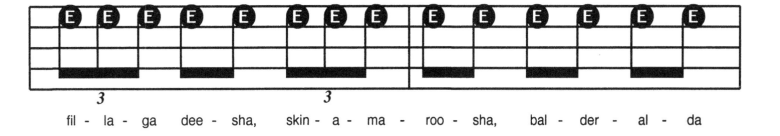

fil - la - ga dee - sha, skin - a - ma - roo - sha, bal - der - al - da

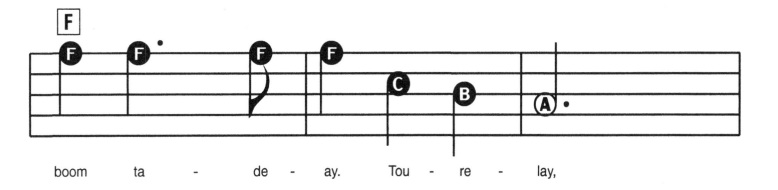

boom ta - de - ay. Tou - re - lay,

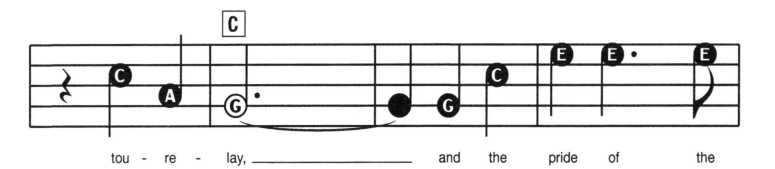

tou - re - lay, _____ and the pride of the

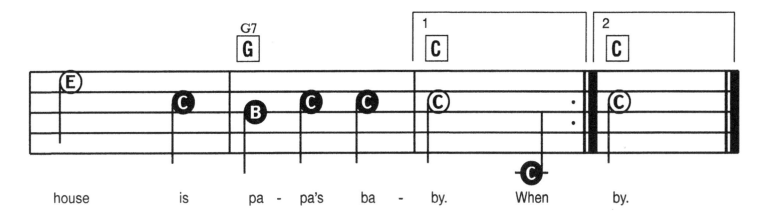

house is pa - pa's ba - by. When by.

The Wearing Of The Green

Registration 9
Rhythm: March

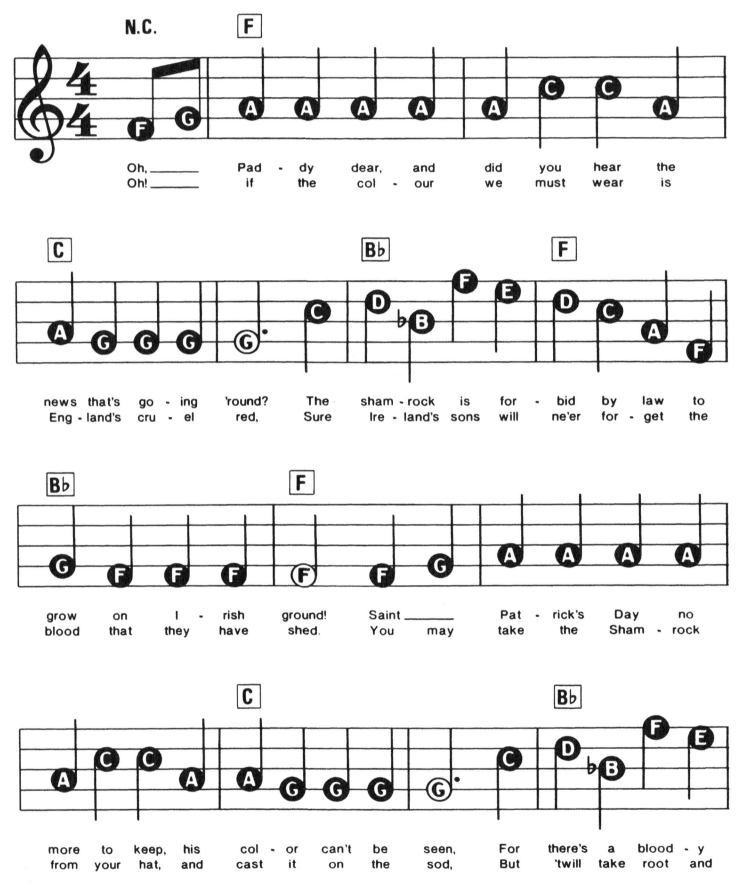

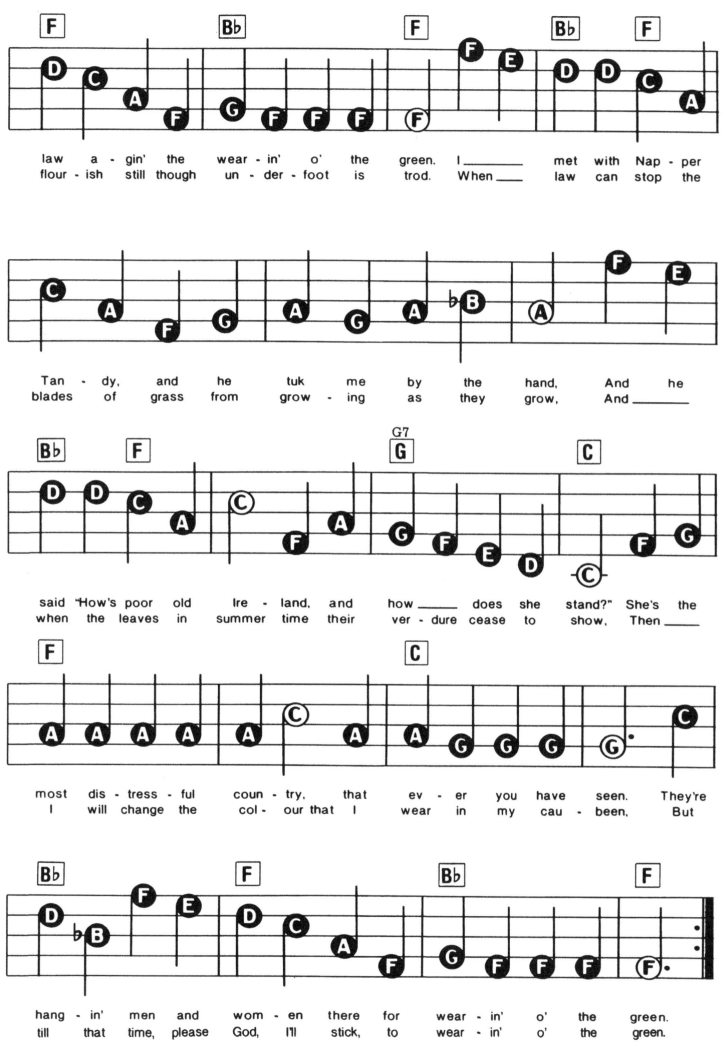

When Irish Eyes Are Smiling

Registration 3
Rhythm: Waltz

Words by Chauncey Olcott and George Graff Jr.
Music by Ernest R. Ball

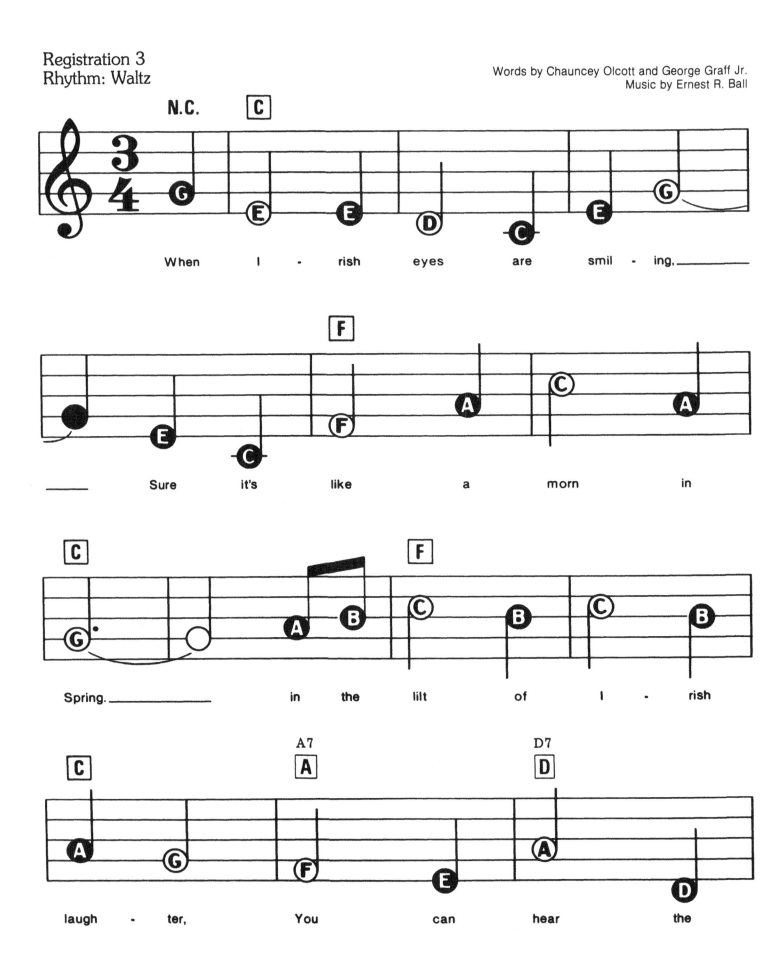

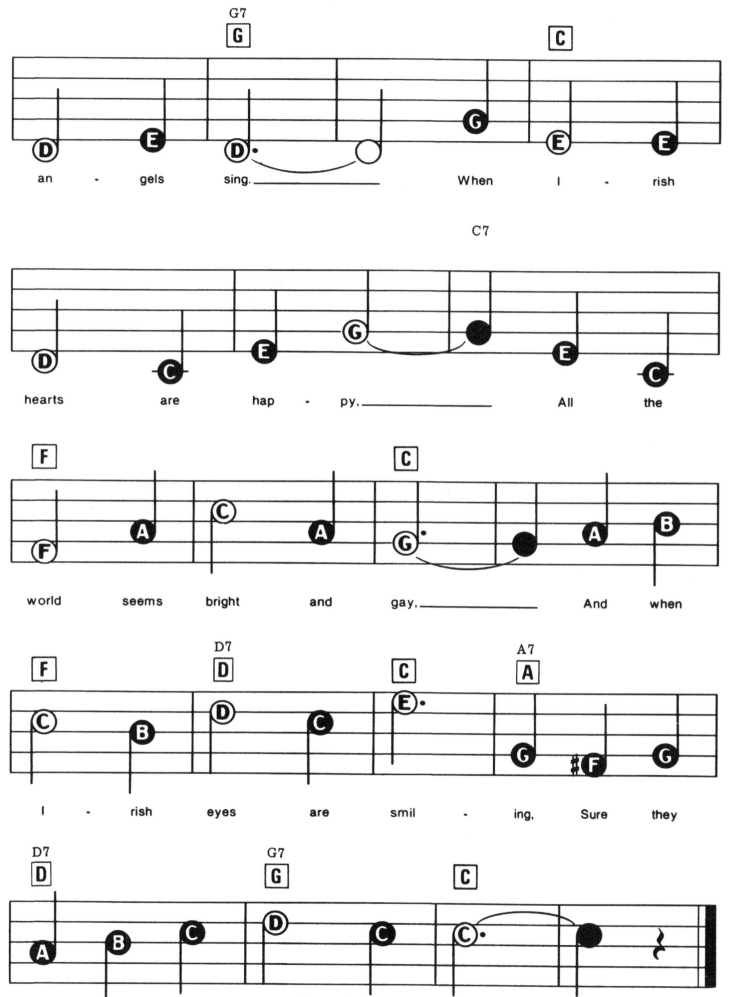

Where The River Shannon Flows

Registration 10
Rhythm: 8 Beat or Pops

Words and Music by
James J. Russell

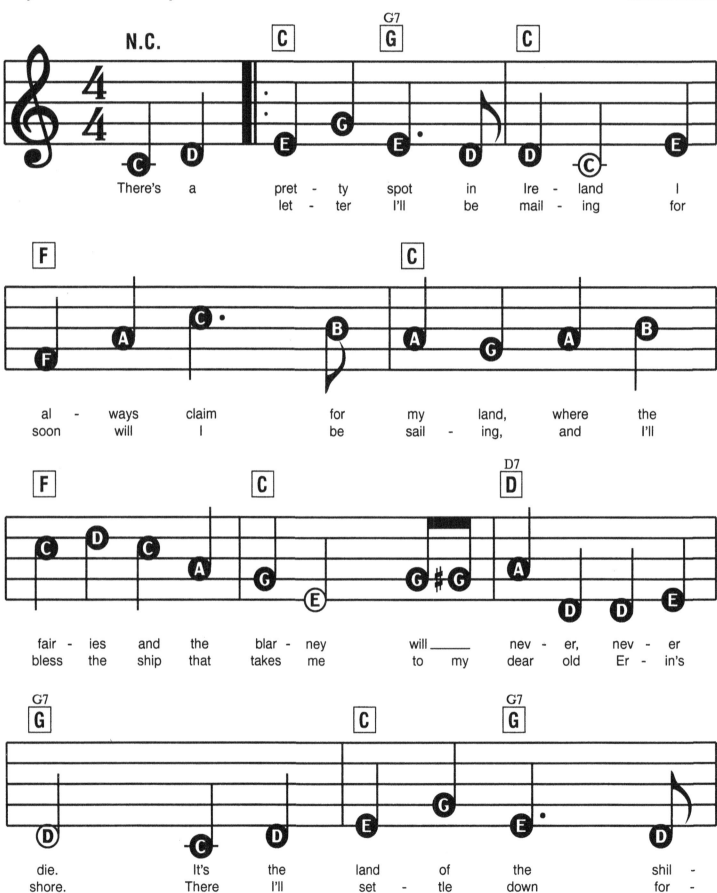

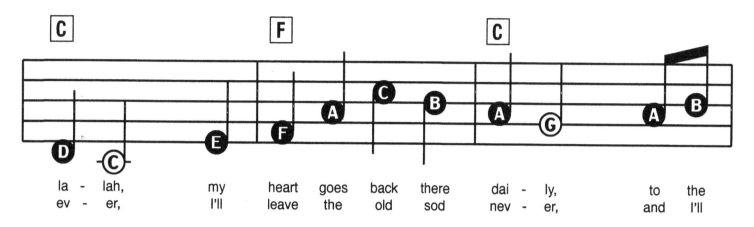

la - lah,   my   heart goes back there dai - ly,   to the
ev - er,   I'll leave the   old   sod nev - er,   and I'll

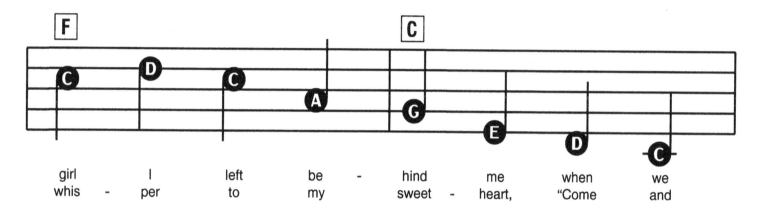

girl   I   left   be - hind   me   when   we
whis - per   to   my sweet - heart, "Come and

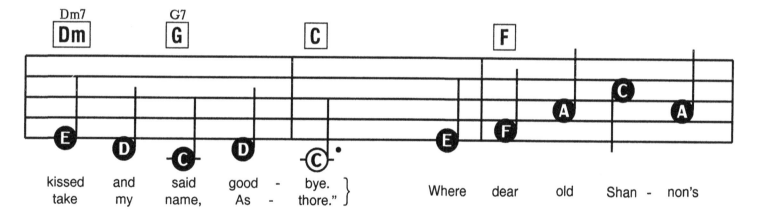

kissed   and   said   good - bye.   Where dear old Shan - non's
take   my   name,   As - thore."

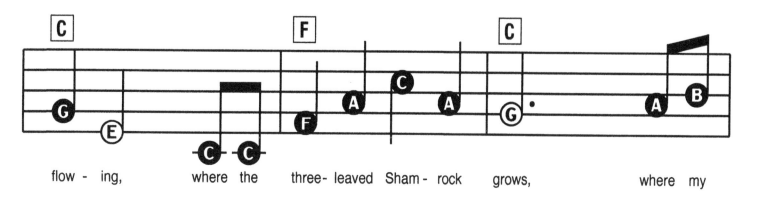

flow - ing,   where the three- leaved Sham - rock grows,   where my

68

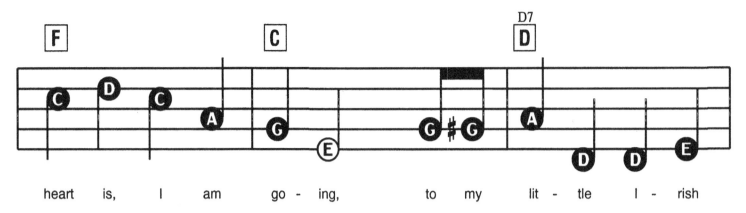

heart is, I am go - ing, to my lit - tle I - rish

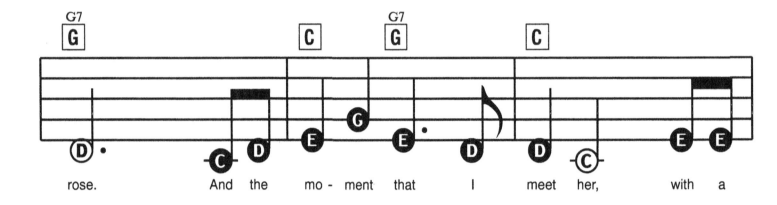

rose. And the mo - ment that I meet her, with a

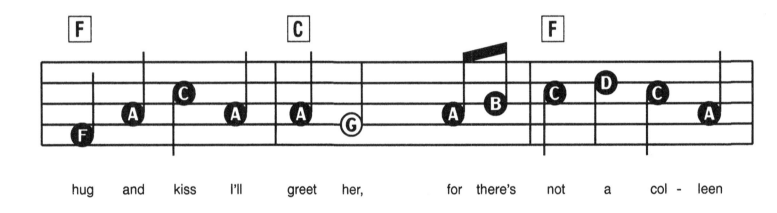

hug and kiss I'll greet her, for there's not a col - leen

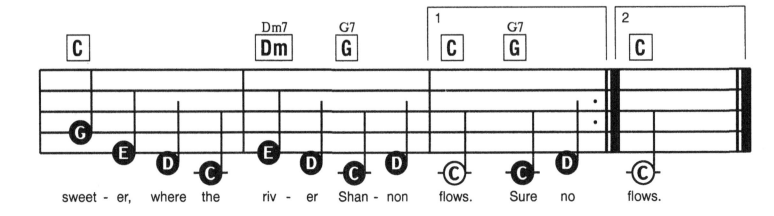

sweet - er, where the riv - er Shan - non flows. Sure no flows.

Who Threw The Overalls In Mistress Murphy's Chowder?

Registration 7
Rhythm: Rock or 8 Beat

Words and Music by
George L. Giefer

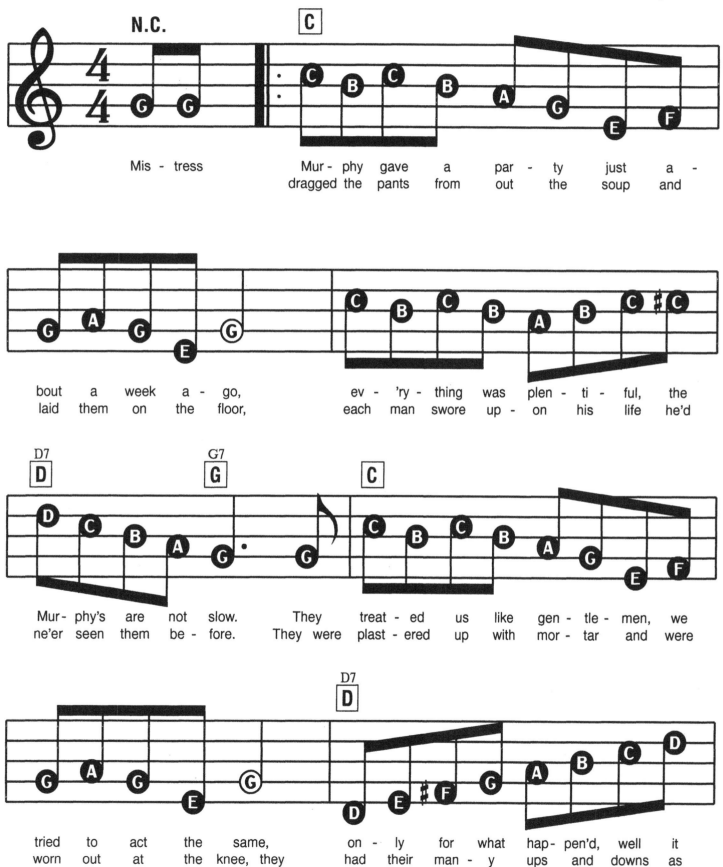

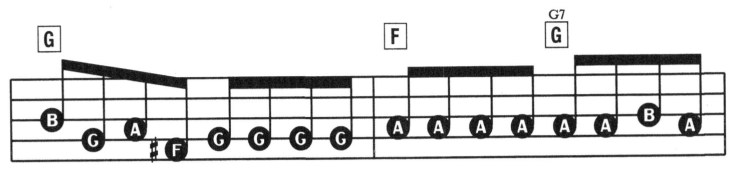

'twas an aw - ful shame, when Mis - tress Mur - phy dish'd the chow - der out she
we could plain - ly see, and when Mis - tress Mur - phy she came to she

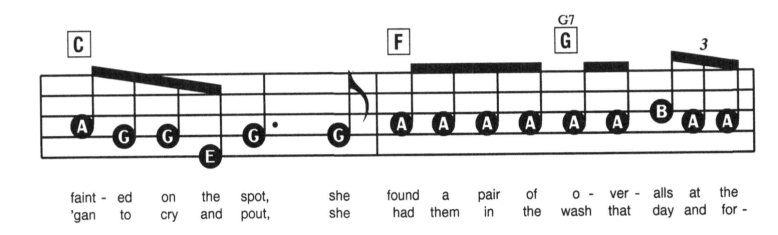

faint - ed on the spot, she found a pair of o - ver - alls at the
'gan to cry and pout, she had them in the wash that day and for -

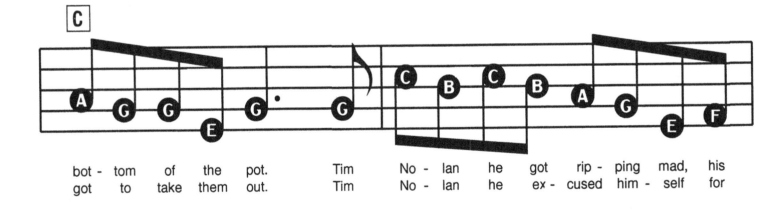

bot - tom of the pot. Tim No - lan he got rip - ping mad, his
got to take them out. Tim No - lan he ex - cused him - self for

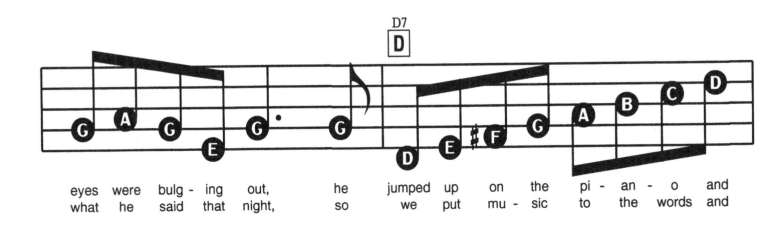

eyes were bulg - ing out, he jumped up on the pi - an - o and
what he said that night, so we put mu - sic to the words and

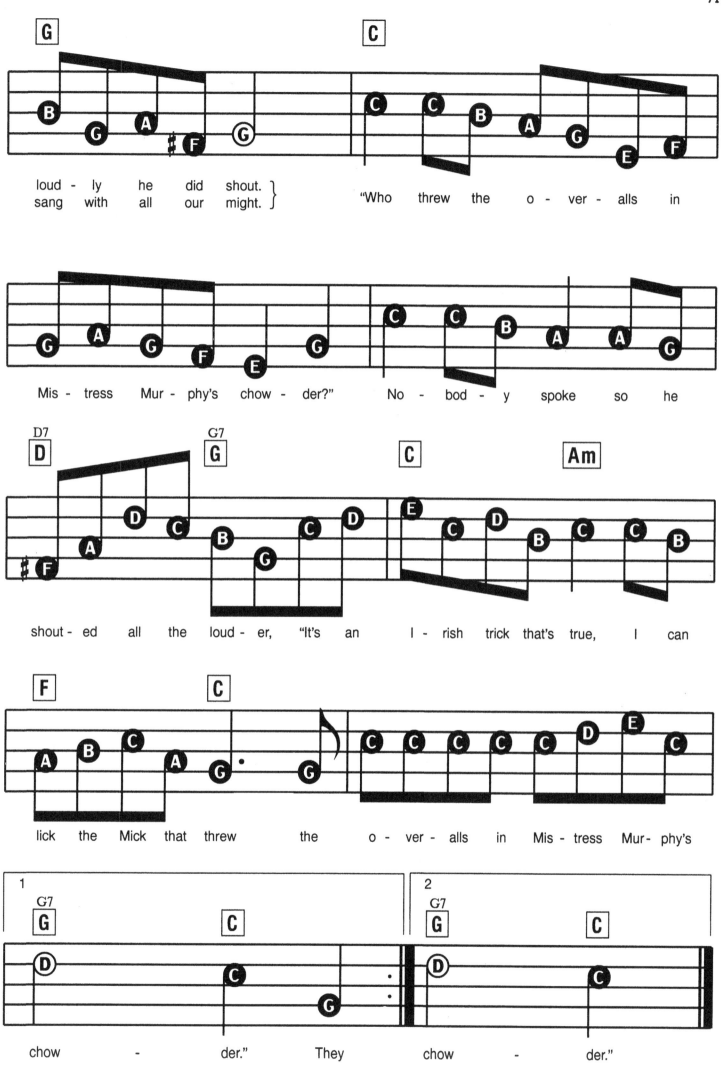

Registration Guide

- Match the Registration number on the song to the corresponding numbered category below. Select and activate an instrumental sound available on your instrument.

- Choose an automatic rhythm appropriate to the mood and style of the song. (Consult your Owner's Guide for proper operation of automatic rhythm features.)

- Adjust the tempo and volume controls to comfortable settings.

Registration

1	Mellow	Flutes, Clarinet, Oboe, Flugel Horn, Trombone, French Horn, Organ Flutes
2	Ensemble	Brass Section, Sax Section, Wind Ensemble, Full Organ, Theater Organ
3	Strings	Violin, Viola, Cello, Fiddle, String Ensemble, Pizzicato, Organ Strings
4	Guitars	Acoustic/Electric Guitars, Banjo, Mandolin, Dulcimer, Ukulele, Hawaiian Guitar
5	Mallets	Vibraphone, Marimba, Xylophone, Steel Drums, Bells, Celesta, Chimes
6	Liturgical	Pipe Organ, Hand Bells, Vocal Ensemble, Choir, Organ Flutes
7	Bright	Saxophones, Trumpet, Mute Trumpet, Synth Leads, Jazz/Gospel Organs
8	Piano	Piano, Electric Piano, Honky Tonk Piano, Harpsichord, Clavi
9	Novelty	Melodic Percussion, Wah Trumpet, Synth, Whistle, Kazoo, Perc. Organ
10	Bellows	Accordion, French Accordion, Mussette, Harmonica, Pump Organ, Bagpipes